You Said **Yes!**

You Said Yes!

Support Materials
for Volunteer
Literacy Tutors

Patricia A. Oliver
Mary L. Wheeler

Heinemann
Portsmouth, NH

Heinemann
A division of Reed Elsevier Inc.
361 Hanover Street
Portsmouth, NH 03801–3912
www.heinemann.com

Offices and agents throughout the world

The authors and publisher wish to thank those who have generously given permission to reprint borrowed material:

Excerpt from "Bookwords: Using a Beginning Word List of High Frequency Words from Children's Literature K–3" by Maryann Eeds from *The Reading Teacher*, 38(4). Copyright © 1985 by the International Reading Association. Reprinted by permission of the International Reading Association.

Excerpt from *Just What I Need* by Bertie Kingore. Copyright © 2005 by Bertie Kingore. Published by Austin: Professional Associates Publishing. Reprinted by permission of the author.

Excerpt from "Reading Orphans" by Steven Layne from *Life's Literacy Lessons: Poems for Teachers*. Copyright © 2001 by the International Reading Association. Reprinted by permission of the International Reading Association.

Excerpt from *Words, Words, Words: Teaching Vocabulary in Grades 4–12* by Janet Allen. Copyright © 1999 by Janet Allen. Reprinted by permission of Stenhouse Publishers.

Library of Congress Cataloging-in-Publication Data
Oliver, Patricia A.
    You said yes! : support materials for volunteer literacy tutors / Patricia A. Oliver,
Mary L. Wheeler.
        p. cm.
    Includes bibliographical references.
    ISBN 0-325-00844-2 (alk. paper)
    1. Reading (Elementary)—Activity programs.   2. Reading—Remedial
teaching.   3. Tutors and tutoring.   4. Literacy programs.   5. Volunteer
workers in education.   I. Wheeler, Mary L.   II. Title.
LB1573.O535 2005
372.41—dc22   2005020045

Editor: Lois Bridges
Production: Patricia Adams
Typesetter: Publishers' Design and Production Services, Inc.
Cover design: Jenny Jensen Greenleaf
Manufacturing: Jamie Carter

Printed in the United States of America on acid-free paper

09   08   07   06   05   VP   1   2   3   4   5

For Tom Potts
For all the volunteers with big hearts
For all emerging and developing readers
For all the educators and administrators working
together to make volunteerism come alive!

CONTENTS

When looking at the ingredients on the label of a can, the one that is listed *first* is the main ingredient. We are going to mention many people in these acknowledgments; however, we want our readers to know that *they* are the main ingredient behind this effort. No worthy thing happens in life unless someone has an idea and pursues it. Empowering literacy volunteers to work with our students is such a worthy thing. There are so many people we need to recognize as this book becomes a reality.

Without the vision of Judy Wallis, language arts coordinator for Spring Branch Independent School District in Houston, Texas, and Lynnda Butorka, her diligent administrative assistant, none of these materials would ever have taken this form. Without the Spring Branch Education Foundation, this effort would not have been funded. Without the support and enthusiasm of our fellow school improvement specialists, we could have lost our momentum.

Our book stands on the strong shoulders of many educators and researchers who proceed our efforts. They include Fountas and Pinnell, Harvey and Goudvas, Marie Clay, John O'Flahavan, and Cris Tovani.

Without the wisdom, expertise, patience, and professional heart of our editor Lois Bridges, and our production editor Patty Adams, we would have been lost. We lift up and salute the inspirational senior citizens from Memorial City Terrace Retirement home and Pines Presbyterian Church who have been our role models for our literacy tutoring programs. Tom Potts, our charter senior tutor, helped so much to plant the idea of using senior citizens in the school as he coined the phrase that his generation is our largest "untapped resource." Sometimes children on the fringes just need the wisdom of and a relationship with an older person who cares about them to let them feel at ease with the written word. And finally, we applaud our husbands and children who have believed in us and have watched these books hatch from dinner conversations to a bound reality. Long live literacy!

Books are to be called for and supplied on the assumption that the process of reading is not a half-sleep; but in the highest sense an exercise, a gymnastic struggle; that the reader is to do something for himself.

—Walt Whitman

Most students master the complex process of reading. They find reading an enjoyable and thought-provoking activity. Enthusiastically embracing the words between the pages of a book, students actively search for meaning in text. Proficient readers rely on their own resources to make sense of the words on the page. Every transaction between themselves and the text results in new beliefs, feelings, and knowledge. These are the students who reach for a book as a matter of habit, not because reading has been assigned.

But for some students, reading is a never-ending gymnastic struggle. We listen as these students somersault, twist, and turn through the pages of a book. We watch as they painstakingly try to find that balance among the letters, words, and meaning on each page. We sigh and shake our heads as they seem to continually bounce off the mat. These are the students who turn the pages and *pretend* to read. These are the students lined up at the nurse's office during silent reading time. They do not connect reading with pleasure. Every time they open the pages of a book, they are reminded that reading is difficult and understanding seems to remain just beyond their grasp.

These readers on the fringe need the added support and encouragement that can be provided by a tutor. Knowledgeable literacy tutors help students discover how to balance the letters, sounds, and words on the page with the meaning of the message. Their presence may mean the difference between a student slipping off the mat and being willing to take another tumble into a book. But in order to ensure that a student who is already confused about the reading process begins to unravel the knots in the rope, a literacy tutor must have the necessary background knowledge.

This book is designed for you, the volunteer literacy tutor. We want you to be excited about your role. The goal for you is to return year after year knowing that you are making a difference in the literacy development of a student. We know that volunteers who feel empowered and validated look forward to the start of the school year. A satisfying experience creates cheerleaders, supportive role models, who go to their churches, neighborhoods, communities, and places of business to recruit more volunteers.

According to the *No Child Left Behind Act,* "Improving the reading skills of children is a top priority for leaders at all levels of government and business, as well as for parents, teachers and countless citizens who *volunteer* at reading programs across the nation." (Italics added by authors.) Volunteer literacy tutors are not certified teachers and therefore should not be expected to take the place of a classroom teacher. But, with explicit training by a qualified supervisor, it is possible to supplement classroom instruction with effective one-to-one tutoring.

The information in this book meets the demands of the National Reading Panel (2000) and *No Child Left Behind*. It addresses the five skills identified by research as critical to early reading success.

1. *Phonemic awareness* The ability to hear and identify sounds in spoken words

2. *Phonics* The relationship between the letters of written language and the sounds of spoken language

3. *Fluency* The capacity to read text accurately and quickly

4. *Vocabulary* The words students must know to communicate effectively

5. *Comprehension* The ability to understand and gain meaning from what has been read

This book provides the theoretical and practical information needed to build a successful, research-based volunteer literacy tutoring program. Chapters 1–5 give you basic information about the reading and writing process. Specific information is given to lay the foundation for a successful tutoring session. Chapters 6 through 8 discuss what to do before reading, during reading, and after reading. This part of the book is packed with additional tools to support a student's literacy journey. The directions for how to establish a personal and academic relationship with a struggling reader are simple, easy to follow, and logical.

The commitment, communication, and community established among the supervisor, the tutor, and the classroom in an effective volunteer literacy tutoring program will help create independent, self-determining readers. Students on the fringe will have the support they need to land on their feet. Working together through the gymnastics of reading can be a meaningful and rewarding experience for the tutor and the student. The information in this book gives you one essential component—the tools for teaching. You will add the second essential component—your time, caring, and commitment!

This practical guide is dedicated to *all* of you in the name of literacy. There is nothing like individual attention in this world. We hope that you find this to be a reciprocal experience—one that volunteers, students, and educators look forward to every week and one in which all lives are touched in unimaginable ways.

Together may each tutor and tutoree:

- enjoy sharing books

- trade ideas

- engage in a variety of genres

- rediscover a vitality in the written word

Comprehension is the thread throughout the process. The sharing of texts will generate writing and soon all on board will be on a voyage that knows no limits! Happy reading!

"A great person is one who has not lost the child's heart."

—Mencius

You Said Yes!

Basic Information
Tutoring Tips

The prospect of spending 30 to 60 minutes with a student may seem a little scary at first. Questions start floating around in your head: Who will I be working with? How will I get to know my student? What will I do to fill all that time? This chapter provides you, the literacy tutor, with answers to these and other questions. The following tutoring tips will help lay the foundation for a successful academic and personal relationship between you and your student. This is the beginning of a wonderful journey!

1. Before you begin teaching, take the time to get to know a little about your student. Ask about her family, friends, teachers, pets, hobbies, favorite books or television shows. Find out what she did last summer, over the weekend, or what she likes to do after school. Encourage her to tell you about hopes, wishes, or dreams. If you are unsure about what to ask, use an interview form (see Appendix A–22, page 88). Learning about the young person you will be sitting next to every week is time well spent!

2. Share your life with your student! He will love seeing pictures of your family, friends, or pets. Tell him about your hobbies. Share your reading world with him. Show him your favorite book. Talk about your favorite author. Bring in and share clippings and pictures from magazines and newspapers. Or, hand your student an interview form and have him interview you! There is a reason for all this talk—the more he talks, the more language he uses and hears, therefore the more language

he learns! Note: This is the same language he will read in books and write in stories!

3. Read aloud to your student.

- Reading aloud to your student is an opportunity for her to hear a fluent, expressive voice. She listens as you share the laughter, tears, mystery, adventure, and excitement that happens between pages of a book.

- The sounds of language can be shared through a read-aloud. She will appreciate the rhyming, playful language in Dr. Seuss' *Cat in the Hat* or Mother Goose.

- Books read to him can be above his reading level. In other words, read books that he would not be able to read independently. Think of the new vocabulary words he will hear! For example, in *Chrysanthemum*, by Kevin Henkes, he will be listening as Chrysanthemum's parents comfort her by describing her name as *beautiful, precious, priceless, fascinating,* and *winsome.*

- You can think aloud about the setting, characters, and plot as you read to your student.

   "Wait a minute. I don't think they are in the house anymore!"
   "I wonder if she's feeling angry because her mother is late."
   "I bet I know what's going to happen next!"

Chapters 6–8 of this book have a plethora of ideas to help you model that little voice in your head that tells you to read, stop, and think.

- There is an additional benefit to reading aloud. Hearing books read aloud provides the student with experience with book language. The language inside books sounds different. For instance, *Once upon a time*, or "said Baby Bear," is language found only in books. Reading aloud to your student builds her understanding of the special language that authors must use to tell their stories.

   You won't have difficulty finding good books for reading aloud. The shelves of your school and public library, as well as your local bookstores are filled with excellent picture books for students of all ages. See Appendix B–1 for examples of popular read-aloud books.

4. Share reading with your student.

▪ During the act of shared reading, your student will follow along as you read. The student must be able to see the text, but you will be providing the voice support by reading out loud. It is critical that your student follow along with her eyes as you read. Sit beside her and arrange the big book page, poem, or chapter book to ensure she can see the words you are reading. For emergent or beginning readers, choose books that have a single line of print on each page with large spaces between the words. Or, use books with repetitive lines or refrains. Point to the words as you read. Instruct your student to "Follow along with your eyes while I read." Don't be surprised when she starts to read along with you!

▪ If your student is reading chapter books, invite him to listen and follow along with his eyes. Two copies of a chapter book make the shared reading time even more powerful. After you have read a few paragraphs, ask him if he would like to read a paragraph. Or combine shared reading with silent, independent reading. After you have read several paragraphs or pages as a shared reading, say to your student, "Let's both read the next few paragraphs silently. We'll talk about them when we're finished." Don't forget to remind him to listen to that little voice in his head as he reads! The little voice refers to the inner conversation a reader has with himself.

▪ Think aloud (marvel at illustrations, make predictions, ask questions, or wonder) while you read. Having your student follow along raises the level of expectation, while still providing the safety of your voice support.

5. Listen to your student read independently. Everything gets better with practice—including reading! Of course, book choice is critical. Either the classroom teacher or you will be responsible for selecting the text for your student. Once the book choice is made, your role is to ensure success by providing just the right amount of support she needs to feel successful. How will you know if the book is the right match? Here is a simple rule to guide your decision: If she is struggling, reading word by word, constantly looking to you to supply the word, or simply mumbling her way through—the text is too difficult. Stop, finish reading it yourself, or put the book aside. Never allow a student to

reach the point of frustration without gently taking over. As she reads independently, you should be there to provide support and to guide her through the tricky parts as long as there aren't too many tricky parts! (In Chapter 2 and Chapter 5, we discuss book choice and specific prompts to support readers.)

6. All reading and no writing? Of course not! All those reading experiences with wild, wonderful, and whimsical words in poems, nursery rhymes, picture and chapter books, go hand in hand with experiences in writing poems, stories, and responses to reading. Sometimes you will be the recorder and write for your student. Depending on her needs, there may be times when you will need to write for her. This gives you the chance to think out loud and show her how to shape a message. For example, stop and say, "Hmmm, I'm not sure what to write. I think I will start at the beginning and read my story again." Rereading your story as you write demonstrates to your student how writers stop and revise words and thoughts. Let her watch as you stop and s-t-r-e-t-ch words to check the spelling. Young students love reading stories written by you! Write about your day at the park, or the day your dog chewed up all your good shoes. Share a memory from your school days, or write down your thoughts about a story you read together.

7. Sometimes you will share the pen, pencil, or marker and write with your student. During shared writing, you and your student will create a message together. Before you begin to write, spend a few minutes talking about the message. Write about her field trip to the zoo, her best friend, her pet, or a character from a book she just read. Once you begin writing, you will be the primary scribe, but encourage her to write as much of the message as she can. If she can only write *I*, or *a*, or *the*—great! Turn the responsibility over to her. Give the student time to write what she knows! Pull out the erasable board if needed and let her try the word first. Help her s-t-r-e-t-ch words, listening for letters and sounds. Again, encourage her to reread as she constructs the message. The poems and stories you construct together will often become a valuable treasure to share with her teacher, classmates, and parents. (Chapter 4 and Chapters 6–8 of this book contain more ideas to support your student's writing.)

8. Give your student time to write independently. Just like reading, when your student is ready, she needs time to write on her own. Independent writing may be in the form of a story or a reader's response. Students

enjoy creating books and stories—big books, rhyming books, poetry books, mysteries, adventures, or autobiographies to name just a few. Or, your student may use a journal or graphic organizer to respond to something just read. Have a reluctant writer? Send home a disposable camera and let her take pictures of her family and friends. This will make a great picture book! Regardless of the age of your student, spend a few moments discussing the message, but give her the responsibility for writing it down. You are there to guide and support. Encouraging her to reread will provide opportunities for noticing anything that needs to be revised. (Chapter 4 is filled with more ideas to build the bridge between reading and writing.)

9. What about phonics? Your student may need support with letters, sounds, and words. But wait a minute! You have already been working with letters and words in reading and writing! *Exactly!* But your student may need additional support. If your student is a beginning reader, she can use magnetic or cut-out alphabet letters to build her name or sight words like *the*, *and*, or *is*. As a developing or transitional reader, she might benefit from sorting words into different categories such as words that end in /ish/ /ing/ or /ight/. (See Chapter 4 for more suggestions to support your student with letters, sounds, and words.) When trying to decide what your student needs, think about going from whole to part to whole. In other words, when you are reading and writing with your student, note what letters, sounds, or word parts that seem to be causing her to stumble. If she doesn't know what to do when she comes across /ing/ /or/ /ed/ or /str/ then grab the erasable board, magnetic letters, or try some word sorts. Then during her independent reading and writing time say, "You can read that word now. Think about what part of that word you know!" You went from her actual reading and writing (*whole*), to focusing on specific areas of need (*part*), to applying what she knows in reading (*whole*).

10. One more tip! Remember, your student has a life *away* from school. Ongoing communication with her parents about who you are and what happens during your time together is a key ingredient for success. If you send home a note and picture of yourself, or make a simple phone call, that support goes a long way!

CHAPTER 2

Reading

It's Okay to Make Mistakes

Think about how you learned to ride a bike, play baseball, or bake a cake. You probably made mistakes. Making mistakes is part of learning. Learning to read is no different. When a reader makes mistakes, he has opportunities to develop his problem-solving skills. Every tutor wants to help; however, jumping in and immediately correcting your student's reading will not create an independent, self-extending reader. Provide support, but let him do the work!

Reading Is a Complex Matter

In order to support your student, you should have a basic understanding of the reading process. Reading is a complex matter, but there are three primary cueing or information systems proficient readers use as they read.

1. the semantic or meaning system (It makes *sense!*)

2. the syntactic or structural/grammatical system (It *sounds* right!)

3. the graphophonemic or letter–sound system (It *looks* right!)

Of course, other things affect the reader such as the genre, text format, or even his surroundings. But for the moment, let's focus on just three cueing systems. Figure 2–1 shows the three cueing systems. The main idea is that all three cueing or information systems work together

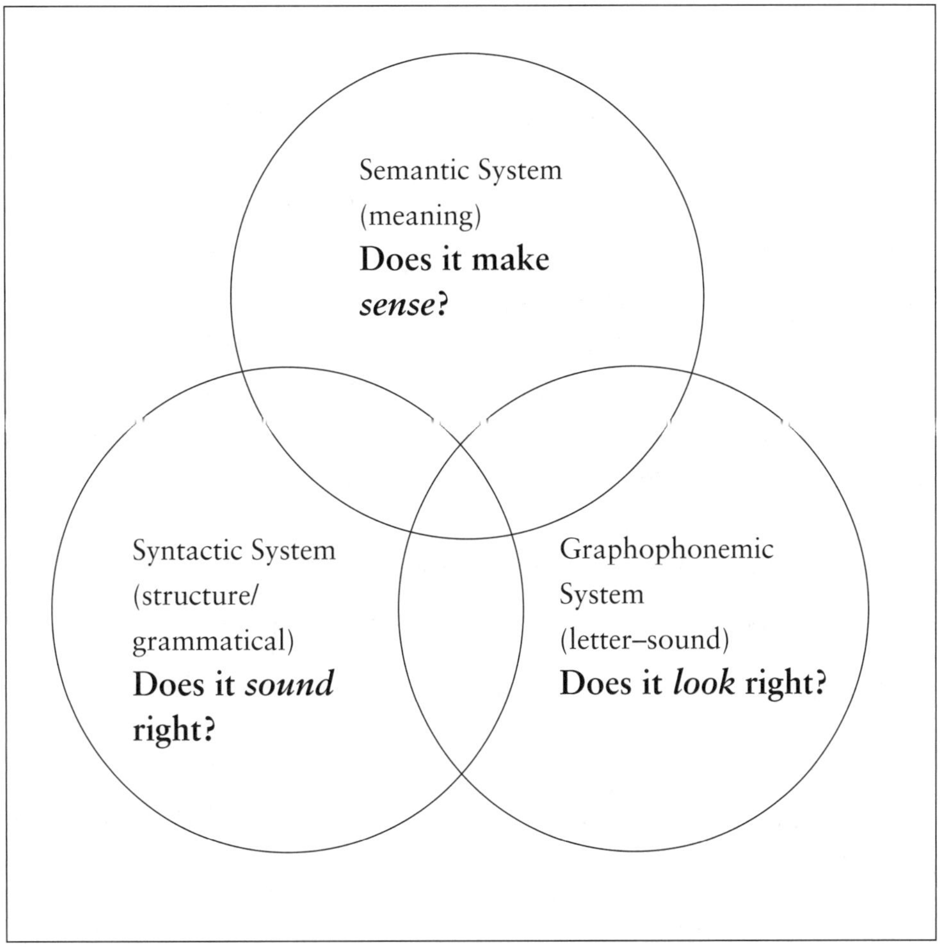

Figure 2–1
Cueing Systems

Semantic System
(meaning)
**Does it make
sense?**

Syntactic System
(structure/
grammatical)
**Does it sound
right?**

Graphophonemic
System
(letter–sound)
Does it look right?

as we read. Read the following sentences and think about what cueing or information system you used to complete the sentence.

1. Everyone blew out the candles and sang Happy _____! (Okay, you knew the next word was *Birthday!* Why? You relied on your background knowledge. You used the semantic or meaning cueing system. It made sense!)

2. This is a snuffling. Here are three _____. (You filled in the word *snufflings*. Why? Even though there is no such thing as a *snuffling*, you used the syntactic system. Your knowledge of sentence structure told you the next word would be plural. It *sounded* right!)

3. The kitten had black, white, and y_____ stripes. (You probably said *yellow*. Why? While you may have used all three cueing systems, you knew the specific color because of the letter–sound information provided by the letter *y*. It *looked* right!)

Your goal as a volunteer literacy tutor is to support and create an active reader who keeps trying and who knows how to work on unknown words in a variety of ways. You want your student to know how to use all three cueing or information systems. The questions inside each circle in Figure 2–1 are prompts that will help your student use different sources of information as he reads. When he comes to an unfamiliar word and makes an attempt, you might say *Did that make sense?* or *Did it sound right?* or *Does that look right to you?* Prompts are critical to creating independent readers. It is best to start off with just a few prompts, and as your confidence builds you can add to your repertoire. The following are a few quick and easy prompts.

- Try that again and think about what would make sense.

- Try that again and think about what would sound right.

- Do you know another word that starts with those letter(s)?

- Do you know another word that ends with those letter(s)?

- Go ahead and start the word and think about what would sound right and make sense.

- Look at the picture.

- You were almost right! Try that again.

- Skip it. Go on to the end, then go back.

Remember when your student makes errors, she has the opportunity to learn how to work out words the way good readers do. Working out errors will help her learn how to read independently. Every time you give your reader time to problem solve when she notices a mismatch between what she read and the text, you support her learning. You guide her toward becoming a strategic reader who won't need to swivel her head toward you every time she comes to an unknown word.

CHAPTER 3

Read It Like the Teacher!

Good readers sound smooth and fluent. The reading rate accelerates as students begin to understand the reading process and become more confident readers. But we should expect and encourage fluent reading right from the beginning. While you are helping your student along the path toward independent reading, don't forget that proficient readers are also fluent readers!

What do we mean when we say, "She's a fluent reader"? Fluent reading involves more than just sounding out every word. In fact, if your student is sounding out every word, she is *not* reading fluently. Fluent reading involves *automaticity*. In other words, she should automatically recall most of the words or know how to quickly figure out unknown words. Fluency also involves changes in the reader's pitch, intonation, stress, attention to natural language, or phrasing. To put it simply—you want your student to "read like the teacher."

There are several ways to improve your student's fluency. One of the easiest ways is by *modeling* fluent reading. Every time you read aloud to your student, you model fluent reading. She will hear the growl as you read "Who's been sitting in my chair?," or the whimsy in your voice as you sing "Who's afraid of the big, bad wolf?" Poems or nursery rhymes are also excellent sources for helping her with fluency. Share a poem together and listen as she mimics the rhythm of your voice. Even older students enjoy the rhythm of poems.

Rereading familiar (previously read) texts is another excellent way to build fluency. Rereading familiar texts allows your student to focus on phrasing or intonation once he is familiar with the words. If your student is older and reading longer texts, he might reread his favorite page or passage. Everyone loves to hear themselves read, so encourage him to tape himself reading. Your student will hear how his oral reading improves every time he rereads. Send the tape home to show his parents how his reading has improved. You might give him a purpose for rereading. Have him tape himself reading a story or poem for students in a primary classroom. Knowing that his taped story or poem is part of another classroom's listening center is bound to bring a smile to your student's face.

There are several other ways to build fluency.

■ *Choral reading.* You and your student read a poem or story together. Always read the text through several times before you ask her to read it with you. This will give her time to hear the rhythm, pattern, and natural language of the poem or story.

■ *Echo reading.* You read a line and have the student immediately repeat the same line. Echo reading works very well with poems. "I'm Thankful," by Jack Prelutsky, is a wonderful example of a poem that works well for echo reading. Read the first verse below and imagine how it would sound as an echo reading.

> I'm thankful for my baseball bat,
> *I cracked it yesterday,*
> I'm thankful for my checker set,
> *I haven't learned to play,*
> I'm thankful for my mittens,
> *one is missing in the snow,*
> I'm thankful for my hamsters,
> *they escaped a month ago.*

■ *Phrase reading.* Read a phrase and ask the student to repeat the phrase.

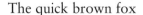

The quick brown fox   jumped over   the lazy dog's back.

■ *Reader's Theatre.* Use a familiar story with or without dialogue and rewrite it as a play. Have your student read the narrator or a character's dialogue. Fairy tales are easy to turn into a Reader's Theatre piece, and no props are required! There are numerous websites that offer Reader's Theatre scripts ready to be downloaded (see http://www.readerstheatre.com).

■ *Familiar readings.* If you are working with a beginning reader, use a story familiar to her. The simple text and story lines are excellent for turning into a Reader's Theatre performance. Have her read the "talking" parts and you read the rest.

As the tutor, you can evaluate your student's reading fluency by listening to her oral reading and asking yourself several simple questions: (1) Does she read in phrases?; (2) Does the reading sound smooth?; (3) Does she change her voice when she sees a question mark or an exclamation point?; and (4) Does she read with expression?

Remember that if a student is struggling to read a book it *will not* help your student learn to read fluently. Any time she is struggling through a text, the material is probably too hard. You might say to her, "I think I chose the wrong book for you. Let's read another one together." Or you might simply stop and read the rest of the story to her. Fast, pleasurable, easy reading will build skills and increase fluency every time!

CHAPTER 4

Reading and Writing Go Hand in Hand

Understanding the mechanics of writing is important. Brainstorming, drafting, revising, and editing, or even creating a story map are just parts of the writing. Writers should be able to answer the question, "Why am I writing this?" In other words, writers need to understand their *purpose* for writing.

So, why do we take time to sit down and compose a message? Writers enjoy writing down interesting words, phrases, or ideas. Writers create shopping lists, lists of things to do, books to read, or ideas for stories. Writers think and compose messages about trips to the zoo, making cookies with mom, learning to ride a bike, or why the character in a book ran away from home. Writers *think* and *write* down their thoughts!

As a literacy volunteer, you have the opportunity to help your student discover authentic reasons to write. Working side by side with your student provides opportunities to demonstrate how people use writing in their daily lives. Sometimes you will compose the message, other times you will write with your student, occasionally passing the responsibility (and the pen) to the student as he puts his own thoughts down on the page. Working one-to-one with your student provides a unique opportunity—every time you meet. There are always new reading and writing activities! So, whether you and your student jot down a list, create a poem, or write a story, a clear message is sent: Reading and writing go hand in hand.

Help students to *think* and *write* during the tutoring session. Here are a few ideas to get you started.

- *Create a list of names.* Write down friends, family members, or characters from the books you are reading. Have beginning readers write the names on sentence strips, cut them apart, and put them back together. Developing and transitional readers can choose a name and write a *snapshot* or a short description of the person on each strip.

- *Create a list of things to buy, or do, holiday or birthday wishes.* These lists can be used later for minibooks.

- *Label diagrams or drawings from a story.* Have students draw their own picture and label it.

- *Compose short notes.* These notes can be memos, greeting cards, postcards, or letters to friends, family, teachers, or book characters.

- *Give your student a disposable camera to take home.* Glue developed pictures on tagboard or heavy paper and staple the pages together—a ready-made book! He will love writing stories about his family and friends using real photographs.

- *Have the student reflect on the tutoring session in a personal journal.* Keeping a personal journal is even more powerful when *you* write in yours at the same time! (Check discount stores for inexpensive journals.)

- Maintain a *reading log* of books your student has read.

- Write *summaries* of stories.

- Draw and fill in *character webs*.

- Complete a *graphic organizer* after reading.

Chapters 6–8 also include a variety of ways to connect reading and writing.

Keep in mind as your student writes, you will have many opportunities to demonstrate a variety of skills and strategies. With your support, he will begin to notice many things as he writes.

- Writing often involves saying words slowly, *s-t-r-e-t-ch-ing* the sounds, and writing the letters, from left to right. Your beginning students will begin to see the connection between the sounds and the letters. (You are teaching some phonics here!)

■ Writers *leave spaces* between words so that the reader can understand the message. If your student forgets to add a space between words, show him how to use his finger or a tongue depressor as a spacer. Draw a face on a tongue depressor and you have Space Man!

■ Writers *think* and *plan* what they want to say. Take a few minutes to brainstorm with your student about her topic. *Talking* is a great way of helping a student plan her writing.

■ Every writer *rereads*, *revises*, and *edits* their writing. Show him one of his favorite read-alouds and explain how the author had to rewrite the story many times before his editor was happy!

■ Writers create text in a particular *form* (letter, note, diary, story), for a specific *audience* (Who am I writing this to?), on a particular *topic* (zoo, picnic, trip to Mexico), and for a particular *purpose* (Why am I writing this?). Authors use the acronym PIE to make the distinction between

　　■ persuading

　　■ informing

　　■ entertaining

Here are a few quick reminders about writing:

1. Spend some time *talking* about the message you are going to write. Talking is part of planning.

2. When you write *with* or *for* your student, make sure he can see what you are writing.

3. Always *model* rereading! The student needs to see that writers always go back and reread their writing.

4. Don't be afraid to *think aloud* as you write. Your student will see that writing *is* thinking. Encourage him to think aloud as he writes.

5. Depending on the age and needs of your student, point out letters, sounds, words, sentence structure, and punctuation in the story.

6. Have fun and celebrate your budding author!

You may be working side by side with a young, emergent reader. So what does he need to learn and how can writing help? First of all, these readers need to learn how to tell one letter from another. Your student may even need to learn letter names along with their forms and sounds. He may not understand that words are made up of sounds that are related to letters or groups of letters. More important, if your student has little experience with the world of literacy, then he won't understand how knowing letters and sounds can help him write and read words.

So how can you help students learn letters? The following are a few suggestions.

- *Make a personal alphabet book.* Staple or bind together tagboard pages to create a blank book. Write one letter of the alphabet on each page. Using stickers, pictures from magazines, or photographs of objects, have your student place one picture on each page whose beginning sounds matches the letter on the page. Always start with letters and sounds he already knows! Completing a personal alphabet book will take several sessions, but it will quickly become a *familiar* book to read aloud at the beginning of each tutoring session.

- *Make letter posters using environmental print.* Focus on the letters he almost knows but still has some difficulty recognizing immediately. Write or glue construction paper cut-outs of a letter in the middle of a piece of poster board. Search for pictures in magazines whose beginning sound

Figure 2–2

matches the letter. Create a collage by pasting the pictures around the letter. Help your student label each picture, encouraging him say the name of each picture slowly, s-t-r-e-t-ch-ing and listening for each letter and corresponding sound. Write any *silent* letters for him thinking out loud, "You know there is one sound you can't hear. Let me fill that one in for you." It is important for children to see words spelled accurately so their brains can record accurate visual images.

So What About Spelling?

It is critical that your student grasps that spelling helps the reader understand what the writer is trying to say. It takes many years for students to develop a large vocabulary of words they know how to spell. There are very few of us who can spell every word in our language. What really matters is that we get better at spelling every time we write. As adults, we usually recognize when a word doesn't *look* right and we search for the correct spelling. We have a repertoire of strategies to uncover the correct spelling, including grabbing a dictionary.

But we all remember the papers dripping with red ink! When thinking about your student's writing, think about what his writing tells you he *can* do. You won't be able to teach him techniques for every problem that comes up in his writing. It is important to focus on what he already knows and pick one or two areas that seem to need the most work.

Help him focus on a few words to fix up. Tell him to circle two or three words that don't look right. Encourage him to try several things: (1) say the word slowly; (2) think about how the word might look; and (3) think about another word like the one he is trying to write. Ask him the following questions. "Do you know any other words that start or end with the same letter(s)?" "Do you recognize any *parts* or *chunks*—like *at*, or *ing*? Are any of the words on your spelling list?" Pull out a dry erase board to write down a similar word to see if that helps. Say to your student, "You can write *bike*. How do you think *like* would look?"

Create a set of *word bank* cards. These cards can be spelling words you have already worked on. Write one word on each 3-inch by 5-inch card. Punch a hole in the corner and keep all the cards on a ring or arrange them alphabetically in a recipe box. As he writes, remind him to check his word bank cards for any words he feels don't *look* right. Or you can also use a manila folder instead of a word bank to record these words. Divide the folder into twenty-six boxes and write one letter of the alphabet in each box (see Appendix A–23, pages 89–90). Help your student keep track of words he can recognize and spell correctly by writing them in the appropriate boxes. Now your student has an individual word wall he can refer to during writing. It is important to hold him accountable for spelling these words correctly.

Remember that student writers do not need to spell everything correctly. One exception might be the Minibooks that beginning readers create as take-home readers. Since these books will be reread many times, words should be spelled correctly.

CHAPTER 5

So Much to Do!
So Little Time!

Whether you plan to tutor for thirty or sixty minutes, the time will fly by. Don't worry about having enough to do with your student. The time intervals in this chapter are only suggestions. After you get to know your student, you will be able to tailor your tutoring sessions to fit his needs.

Reading *to*, *with*, and *by* Students
(Ten to Twenty Minutes)

The possibilities for reading aloud or to your student are endless. This is a time when your student can sit back and enjoy listening to a fluent, expressive reader. There are ABC books, nursery rhymes, picture books (fiction and nonfiction), or special books you bring in from home. You might read something interesting like a newspaper or a magazine. Share your reading world with him! The age of your student will determine what type of reading material will be appropriate, but he will definitely enjoy knowing you are a reader, too.

Talk and think aloud as you read. Access that little voice in your head. In other words, have a *conversation* about whatever you are reading. The following are a few prompts when thinking aloud.

■ This makes me think of . . .

■ I wonder what will happen next?

■ Why do you think (the character) did that?

■ I wonder how (the character) feels.

■ Why do you think the author wrote this story or article?

■ I think this word means . . .

Sitting next to a caring adult and listening to nursery rhymes, poems, or stories may not be a daily experience for some of these students. As the tutor, the time you spend reading *to* your student may become the most valuable and enjoyable part of the tutoring session. Not only is there pure joy in reading aloud, you will also be modeling fluency, sharing new vocabulary, and demonstrating the skills and strategies of proficient reading. One word of caution—it's important to use the read-aloud time to teach, but teach *lightly*. Listening to and enjoying a story should be the main focus!

During this time in the tutoring session, you might also spend time reading *with* your student. While the read-aloud material may be above his reading level, the material you choose to read with your student will probably be something he can read with your support. When reading with your student, sit beside him and make sure he can see the text as well as any illustrations. Ask him to follow along with his eyes as you read the text. If your student is a beginning reader, use material with large print and wide spaces between the words. Point to each word as you read. When it is appropriate, invite your student to read along with you during repeated lines or phrases. Don't be surprised if he starts reading without an invitation! After the first reading, ask him to point out words, letters, or any punctuation you have been emphasizing.

If your student is older and reading more challenging material, having two copies of the book makes it easier for her to follow along as you read. Stop occasionally and ask her if she would like to read. If she starts reading independently, great! Let her continue reading or take turns. As you read together, stop and talk. Think aloud about the setting, characters, or plot.

Once you've set the tone by reading *to* and *with* your student, he needs time to reread familiar text. Familiar reading builds success. It also provides an opportunity to develop vocabulary and sight word recognition fluency. If your student is a beginning reader, a selection of familiar books pulled from his individual reading box will give him several book choices. An older student may choose to reread a favorite page or paragraph. Chapter books provide a perfect opportunity to point out how proficient readers often reread previously read pages. Rereading is a critical strategy! Explain that even adults reread to enjoy or make sense of texts. Keep a few favorite poems handy for rereading. Poems are a short, but an enjoyable way to ensure familiar reading for all ages.

Reading a new book or chapter is probably the most important activity in the tutoring session. This is an opportunity for your student to apply and practice the skills and strategies of proficient reading. Your role as the tutor is to provide support through prompts and conversation to help the student through unfamiliar material. Choosing the new book will require that you determine: (1) the difficulty level of the new text, (2) how to introduce the book to the student, and (3) how to provide the most effective support.

Difficulty Level

A critical factor for your student's success is the difficulty level of the new text. A student's success with a new book may be affected by unfamiliar words, interest, background knowledge, or even the format of the text (small print, no illustrations, subheadings, or long chapters). Rule number one: *The new book should be a good match for the student*. Too many unfamiliar words create frustration for the reader. If she is stumbling over the words, the text's meaning will break down. As soon as you observe the student's frustration with the new text, stop reading. Simply say, "Maybe we chose the wrong book today," or "Why don't you let me read for awhile." If it's an enjoyable chapter book, change it to a read-aloud book. You can read it to her. Don't worry if you discover the new book you have chosen is too hard. Many experienced teachers have realized halfway through a book that it didn't match the child. When choosing a new book, ask,

■ Is there any repetitive language to help my beginning student? How many lines of print are on the page? Is the print large enough? Are there wide spaces between the words?

■ Will my student understand the concepts and vocabulary in this text?

- Are the chapters too long? Too short?

- Do the illustrations provide enough support?

- Are there charts or diagrams that might be confusing?

- Will my student enjoy reading this particular genre?

Introducing the Book

They way you introduce a new book to the student will depend on the student's needs and type of text. With beginning readers, your introduction to a book may be more active. You might read the title, look at the illustrations, and have your student predict what he thinks the story will be about. Pointing out pictures, words, or repetitive phrases as you preview the book will set up the meaning of the story and make the initial reading more successful for the student. Ask him to "find the word *and*," or repeat a phrase like "he huffed and he puffed and he blew the house down!" Gradually turn the responsibility of becoming familiar with the book over to your student. Encourage him to look at the pictures and predict what the story will be about. Give him time to look through a nonfiction book then ask, "What do you think you might learn as you read this book?"

Remember the purpose of this type of book introduction is to build background knowledge. Developing or transitional readers will benefit from this kind of initial work. Model for the reader how good readers take time to read the title and thumb through the pages to check out the print size and illustrations. Many of the books at this level have front or back covers that give a brief summary of the book. Encourage students to read these blurbs. Looking at chapter titles and subheadings in chapter books will also help the student gain insight into the new material. Make sure your student has enough background information to help make the first reading as successful as possible. The student will have more cognitive energy or brain power to focus on unfamiliar words or phrases if they already have a basic understanding of the text.

When starting a book introduction ask,

- What is the a purpose for reading the text? Say, "Please read and find out what happens to (character)," or ask, "Why don't you read and tell me what happens after a spider spins the web?"

- What do you know about this topic?

- What do you think is going to happen on the next page? Next chapter?

- What is happening in this picture?

- "Can we read this tricky part together?"

Providing Support

Your student needs opportunities to demonstrate what he knows about the reading process. If you jump in the minute he comes to an unfamiliar word, you send the message, "You can't do this by yourself!" When your student makes a mistake, give him some wait time. Waiting three to five seconds gives him the chance to solve the problem himself. If he still seems confused, provide support by asking, *Start the word and think about what would make sense. Does any part of the word look familiar?* or *What part of that word do you know?*

It is not easy to decide when to step in and when to give the student time to problem solve. As a rule of thumb, ignore errors that do not change the meaning of the story. Proficient readers make these types of errors all the time. If your student makes an error that does change the meaning, remember to wait at least until the end of the sentence to see if he self-corrects. Stop him only at a few key places. Teaching at too many places will only cause confusion. Remember, if he is struggling with too many words, the text is probably too hard and you should intervene and take over. Sometimes it is okay to tell your student the word. If he's reading about dinosaurs, the phrase *Tyrannosaurus Rex* is not worth spending time on! Simply give him the word and, if necessary, a quick explanation. It is more important to allow your student to continue reading. Meaning is lost when he must spend time problem solving words that may be above his reading level.

Don't forget to praise your student! Always give her positive feedback about her reading. Your student may not have experienced much success in reading. A key part of your role is to encourage her to reflect on her reading and celebrate her successes! You might say,

- "I liked the way you figured out that word by yourself!"

- "What helped you figure out that word?"

- "I noticed you reread when it didn't make sense."
- "You sounded just like the teacher when you read that!"

Letter–Word Work (Five Minutes)

Fluent readers recognize words immediately or have the tools to figure things out for themselves. During word work time your student will have time to practice on letters, sounds, or words. The activities you choose will depend on your student's age and needs. Your beginning reader can create his own alphabet book, sort letters, or build words with magnetic letters. Erasable boards provide opportunities to write letters or words in a novel way. Your student will love playing a word or letter game such as *Go Fish* or *Concentration* with sight words.

Your developing or transitional reader can do word sorts and search for spelling patterns. Give him a list of multisyllabic words and ask him to sort for words that have the same spelling pattern. Create a word bank of vocabulary words using a recipe box and 3-inch by 5-inch cards. Your student will enjoy playing Wordo, which is similar to Bingo except that boxes are filled in with sight words, vocabulary words, or spelling patterns. Keep in mind that what your student demonstrates as he reads the *new* text will often determine what you focus on during this part of the tutoring session. See the photograph on the following page for a letter-word activity.

Writing (Ten to Fifteen Minutes)

There are a myriad of activities to use during writing time. If you are making an alphabet book with your student, keep going. It will take several tutoring sessions to create an alphabet book, so don't worry if this time blends into the writing time. Your younger student will enjoy creating a minibook he can take home. All you need are a few pages stapled together, stickers, pencil, and you are ready to go! The more beginning the reader, the more simple the story line—the book might have just one sticker at the top of the page, one sentence at the bottom. This is a perfect opportunity to demonstrate how good readers and writers reread before they continue!

During this time, encourage your student to write about what they know. The younger the student, the more you need to share the pen as he constructs text. When you share the pen, you encourage him to write the letters, sounds, or words he knows while you write the rest. For instance, he may want to write about one of his friends. Construct the message together by saying, "Maybe we could write, 'My friend likes to play games with me.' " Have your student s-t-r-e-t-ch words by repeating them slowly and writing any letter and sounds he hears. You fill in letters and sounds he doesn't yet recognize.

Your older students can use a response journal to jot down thoughts, ideas, connections, or predictions about the story or chapter they read. A simple spiral notebook works fine for a response journal. Completing a story map or graphic organizer can also become part of your students' writing time.

Keep in mind the times given for reading, word work, and writing are just suggestions. There may be days when you focus more on one part of the lesson than another. As you get to know your student, it will be easier to determine where you should spend most of your time.

The How and What of Volunteer Tutoring

Before *Reading Activities*

How to Use the Remaining Chapters

The next few chapters are designed to provide tools to use when working side by side with students. Each page explains an explicit aspect of the reading process. It is divided into three sections:

- Before reading (Chapter 6)

- During reading (Chapter 7)

- After reading (Chapter 8)

It may seem odd that reading is a multistep process, but that's because you do it subconsciously. Good readers, like yourself, do an overview of a text before reading. This sets up a purpose for reading. And while you're reading, you're thinking about what you're reading and how you feel about it. When you get stuck or confused, you go back and reread at that point of confusion. And when you're finished reading, you generally talk to someone about what you've read. You also store that text and its reverberations in your brain. These practices matter. Your job is to teach and model these practices of good readers.

Writing is the natural extension of reading. The last section of this part contains ideas for follow-up activities so the fun doesn't stop when the text ends.

Holding Hands with the Author

If a reader is *truly* reading a text and is actively engaged, then she is holding hands with the author. This is a memorable way to show readers how to maximize the reading process.

Try this:

Tutor: *Hold up your right hand. This is the author. Repeat after me: "Yeah author! Wave! You are published! You have something you want me to read and think about! You've worked hard on your piece and you can't wait for me to read it!"*

Student: *(Repeats, probably giggles)*

Tutor: *Now hold up your left hand. This is you—the reader. Let's be honest. Sometimes when you read, or anybody reads for that matter— even the President of the United States—your mind wanders. You are hot, cold, tired, hungry, thirsty, worried, distracted. Basically, you are preoccupied. You may look like you're reading, but you are not thinking!*

    (Bring hands together as if clapping and intentionally miss) This is what happens when readers read without thinking. (Have student mimic) Now! Hold up that left hand again. Remember, this is you, the reader! Each finger represents something a good reader does. (Wiggle each finger as you emphasize each explicit aspect.) Your thumb monitors meaning. Make sure you can summarize as you go! Your index finger stands for asking questions. Your middle finger makes inferences. Your ring finger visualizes the text. Your pinky finger determines importance. The palm of your hand makes connections of this text with other texts and life experiences. It takes all of these working together simultaneously for a full reading experience. (Interlace fingers and place them on top of your head. Have the student do the same.) Now, when you are truly holding hands with the author, do you see what happens? All of that thinking sifts down into your brain and your thoughts can come out of your mouth so we can have conversations with other readers! And that is what reading is all about! Ready to begin? Let's shake on it!

Your Brain Is Like a Pantry!

This is one exercise to show students how much information our brains hold. Do it before reading any text, fiction or nonfiction.

Tutor (to student): *So, close your eyes and tell me, if you were to go to your pantry, or food cabinet, and open the door right now, what would you see? Pastries? Spaghetti noodles? Cans of soup?*

Student: I see _____ . . . (*tutor listens patiently, nods and prompts when necessary*)

Tutor: *Okay, open your eyes. Tell me, how come you know what is in your pantry at home, but you're sitting here with me right now?*

Student: *Because, I go there all the time! I get hungry every day and I know right where to go to find what I need.*

Tutor: *Wow! Your brain is just like your pantry! It stores all kinds of images and knowledge and memories! So, before we read, we need to visit our "pantry" to see what we know about how this text is set up and what it will be about.*

Rather than just diving into a book, it is critical to access a reader's **schema,** *which is what they already know about a text format or a subject area. For young readers it means taking a book walk or a preview to provide a framework for the story line. A book walk builds interest and motivation. Pictures are used to scaffold understanding and make predictions. Readers can skim for problematic words and capitalize on prior knowledge so they will not be doing a cold read. It's always good to start with questions such as, "What do you think this is going to be about?" or "What do you already know about this topic/genre?" This quick exercise helps build confidence and more "food for the reader's pantry."*

Good Readers Set a Purpose *Before* Reading

Tutor: *So, why are you reading this today?*

Student: *Because I have to!* It's an assignment!

Tutor: *Okay . . . I see that . . . but why else? You know, I read a lot of things every day. When I drink my coffee in the morning I like to look at the headlines. Then I'm reading to be informed, to learn what's going on. Then I turn to the comics . . . I read those for pure entertainment!*

And when I turn to the editorial page, I'm reading to see all the different sides of an issue, like whether kids should wear uniforms to school. I like to see what other people think. I have to do this when I vote . . . I need to read to see the candidates' viewpoints!

Later this afternoon I'm thinking of going to the bookstore. I'm going to spend some time looking for the just right *book for me right now!*

And tonight I have book club. So I'm going to spend some time today rereading the book I just finished. I want to flip back through it, reread the first page, the last page, and go through it to refresh myself on anything that was fuzzy.

So . . . let's take a closer look at what you're reading today and why you are reading it! Good readers do this every time they read!

The purposes of reading are:

- to practice fluency and reading with expression

- to learn something new (read slowly and monitor comprehension)

- to enjoy

- to see if it is a "just right" book for you

- to compare it to another book or another author

- to get ready for a book club discussion

- to reread areas that were fuzzy

- to analyze the author's style

- to create detailed word pictures in your mind

Smorgasbord Reading

Picture yourself sliding your tray down the line at Luby's cafeteria. Imagine if all you ever had heaped on your plate was mashed potatoes. Pile after pile, bite after bite . . . a predictably soft and bland diet of mashed potatoes for every meal day after day . . . boring, right?

Some of our young readers are stuck in a rut of reading the same type of book over and over again. It is safe, but it is stifling! As readers move into chapter books, they shift more and more from learning to read to reading to learn. Print is all around them and there for the taking—let's capitalize on it!

Part of our job as literate role models is to give their taste buds something new and exciting in print. We need to be like the sample-giver in the store, providing irresistible tidbits of other genres. Before asking them to read, we ought to include something from our world of print that catches our interest. We cannot underestimate our influence in their lives. Consider the following sources:

- An interesting newspaper article

- A comic strip

- A take-out menu with fabulous descriptions of mouth-watering food

- A paragraph from a book we're reading that gives an awesome description

- A poem

- Our favorite picture books from when we were younger

- A pamphlet from an interesting place you've visited

- Anything you've written

It is important to share our passion for print. It is contagious and impacts students' selections as they go through the Luby's cafeterias of print in their lives!

The *Just Right* Book

Everyone knows the story of the *Three Little Bears*. Goldilocks found the porridge to be too hot, too cold, or just right. Same thing with the chairs . . . too hard, too soft, and just right! So that phrase "just right" connects with a smiling nod in all of our brains.

The same rings true with reading. One of the most powerful demonstrations we can do as adults is to share with our students books from each category in our own lives. So here is *your* assignment as a tutor!

Perhaps you have an old physics book at home. Dust it off. Check out the small font, the technical jargon, and the complexity of thought.

Wow! That definitely goes in the *too hard* category! How about that easy book you read on the beach last summer—the one you whizzed through and enjoyed tremendously, but didn't tax your brain too much. That would be in the *too easy* category. Now, select a text that makes you think—one that makes you go back and reread for clarification. It's the one you're recommending to your friends. That is the *just right* book to bring. Share all three books with your student. Talk about what puts them in each category. Then as you work together, begin identifying each text with the three bear language of *too hard, too easy,* or *just right*.

As readers in the wild, we encounter all kinds of texts. We adjust our pacing and our purpose accordingly. Our job is to help kids identify the level of book they are reading and to select texts that are just right for them rather than those that are comfortable and too easy, or those that are way too hard, but look impressive!

FLIP!

It is said that you should never judge a book by its cover. So, we need to somehow quickly figure out if a text can be read independently. How do we know whether we have found just the right book?

Try the FLIP approach!

F = *Friendliness* (does the text seem user-friendly as you flip through?)

L = *Language* (skim a few pages—does the vocabulary seem age appropriate?)

I = *Interest* (there are so many things to read—is *this* an area of interest?)

P = *Past knowledge* (does the reader know enough about the topic/genre?)

This is what good readers do. They flip through the pages and ask the questions about *friendliness, language, interest*, and *past knowledge*. Some readers like to keep a bookmark with "FLIP" written on it as a reminder of this practice.

The Five Finger Rule

When checking out the appropriateness of a text, you can use the five finger rule. Turn to a page with a lot of text. Skim through it carefully, concentrating more on vocabulary than content. Hold up one finger for every unknown word. If you hold up all five fingers, chances are this text is too hard!

Taking a Book Walk

Taking a book walk is known as *previewing the text*. This two-minute exercise prepares the reader for the text. It is just like when we wake up in the morning and think about our day and what to wear. We dress accordingly. If we're going to clean the garage, our outfit looks very different than if we're going on a picnic or going to a wedding. We get ready because we know what to expect. The same is true for reading different genres. Taking a book walk provides a time to:

- Peruse

- Browse

- See how it's organized

- Look at the pictures, photographs, and captions

- Identify genre

- Make predictions

- Locate tricky or exciting vocabulary

- See the author's purpose

- Get comfortable with the format

Here's an example of an exchange:

Tutor: *(with genuine enthusiasm) Whoa, cool! Look at this book we're going to read today! I think you're going to like it a lot! Let's check it out before we read it. That's what good readers do! What can we tell by the cover? The title? What's the voice inside your head thinking before we even open it up?*

Student: *(Makes a prediction or a connection . . . says something)*

Tutor: *(Gives credence to the student's thought and continues to ask guiding questions) What do you think we'll see when we turn the page? (If the text is nonfiction, pay attention to the table of contents, the index, the large font headings, and highlighted vocabulary. If it's fiction, have the student turn the pages and comment on what is happening in the story line according to the pictures.)*

During Reading Activities

Read, Stop, *Think!*

Some people believe that reading means buzzing right through the text at breakneck speed, stopping after the last period, sighing, and saying, "I'm done!" The focus for these readers is on finishing. They are cheating themselves of literary opportunities!

Reading is not a race. It is an interactive process, even when we are alone with a piece of text.

Good readers listen to that little voice in their head. It vibrates like a cell phone, alerting them that there is a personal response to what they've read. Whether we read silently or out loud, *if* we are reading carefully, then we are monitoring our understanding. We could be thinking about:

- *Unknown Words.* "Gee, I've never seen that word before! What could it mean? How do I pronounce it? Do I recognize a root word, suffix, or prefix? How can I use the context to decipher its meaning? Maybe I should read on and see if it becomes clear, or go back and try it again."

- *New Information.* "Wow, this is interesting information. I want to remember this! Think I'll highlight it."

- *Something Confusing.* "Time to keep the characters straight. There are too many of them and I am getting confused. Think I'll keep track of them on a bookmark."

■ *Connections.* "Whoa! This reminds me of a time when . . . " or "This reminds me of something else I've read . . . " or "This really happened in the world!"

■ *Predictions.* "I bet I know what's going to happen next."

■ *Inferences.* "Now the author didn't come right out and say it, but when I read between the lines, this is what I'm thinking . . ."

■ *Opportunities to Visualize.* "Even though there are no illustrations here, I can just picture how she looks from the author's description!"

■ *Author's Style.* "Whoa, what a great way to express that thought. Super word choice. I'd like to remember that, so that when I write I can try that style!"

Making Connections

Nothing exists in isolation. Our brains don't take in information and have separate compartments with locked doors. Every time we read, our brains are hard at work. They are busy associating, accumulating, sifting, sorting, comparing, agreeing, disagreeing, and thinking. As readers, we have to make connections with the text.

There are three types of connections that naturally occur while we are reading. While it is not necessarily a priority to label each one, it is important to sift through them and determine which ones are adding to our ability to better understand the text.

Text-to-Text Connections

■ "Hmmm . . . this reminds me of something else I've read!"

■ "Here is a fantasy story about dragonflies that get stuck in a Venus Fly Trap plant and here is a factual article on the Venus Fly Trap. Cool!"

Text-to-Self Connections

■ "I know exactly how this character feels. Something similar happened in my life (my school, my family, to my friend . . .)."

Text-to-World Connections

■ "Whoa! This story about bullying and terrorism reminds me of 9/11."

Say Something

Reading is not an underground activity. Though most people read silently with an occasional chuckle, tear, or "aha!," text is meant to be shared. Tutors and teachers have the unique opportunity to talk with students about print. It's a good idea to use a little sticky note or create a stop sign to insert periodically throughout a piece of text to initiate discussion. There are no right answers or things to say, it's just important to react to the text. Here are some ideas:

- Make a connection: to text, to self, to world
- Ask a question
- Tell what this makes you think about
- Make a prediction
- Give a one-sentence summary
- Read your favorite part
- Pick out a favorite phrase or word
- Ask for clarification
- Explain the picture in your head from a particular passage
- React . . . do you agree? Disagree?
- Comment on the author's style
- Tell what you think another character might be feeling
- Share the most important thing about what you just read
- Make an inference

Listen with a careful ear. Let the other person's thoughts noodle into your head and comment on them before sharing your own. This is the BIF (brief, intensive, frequent) way of letting that little voice in your head speak to another little voice.

Say Something Card Prompts

Having the Say Something prompt cards visible as you read together will prompt pertinent BIF (brief, intense, frequent) discussions that will heighten and deepen the shared reading experience (see Figure 7–1).

Figure 7–1 Stop/Ask a Question Chart

The most important thing is to verbalize our thoughts as we're reading. Talking through the fuzzy parts moves comprehension to synthesis!

Inferences

Authors intentionally don't come out and state all of the facts and feelings on a page. They rely on the reader to read between the lines, or to *infer* information from the text. It is important for readers to practice and verbalize this skill from the earliest stages of reading. Here are some examples of what a reader could say.

1. *The text states:* "Mom bolted through the kitchen door, threw the groceries on the counter and ignored the ringing phone." *The reader infers* that Mom was in a hurry, though the text doesn't explicitly state that. The reader might also infer that Mom was late, preoccupied, or angry. Additional details will clarify these ideas.

2. *The text states:* "Harry stepped into his cabin to meet his new roommate. *Thump!* Harry tripped over an open suitcase on the floor. Around the room lay dirty clothes and piles of orange peels." *The reader infers* that Harry's roommate is a messy person.

Good readers use evidence from the text to make inferences. They check themselves as the text continues to see if their inferences hold true.

The Reading Continuum

Imagine yourself driving. The sun is out and the highway is empty. You are going to stay on it for a long time. You turn up the tunes, put it on cruise control, and la dee dah, driving is easy!

Uh oh! Clouds gather, thunder cracks, and within moments hail is pelting down all around you. Roads are slick and the fog rolls in an opaque wave. Time to sit up staight! Reduce your speed. Grip the wheel tightly and concentrate really hard. This driving is tough!

The same thing is true of reading. We encounter all kinds of print. Sometimes we can zip through it. Cruise. Other times it takes tremendous concentration. It's important for a reader to know where they are on the continuum and what their goals and purposes are so they can use the most effective strategies!

Difficult Texts	*Easier Texts*
Read slowly.	Relax!
Take notes.	Read fast!
Monitor your understanding.	Enjoy the ease!
Go back to the confusing part.	Wallow in the pictures!
Keep a bookmark.	

Visualizing

Making Pictures in Our Heads as We Read

You know the author has done a good job when you feel that movie projector rolling in your head creating images on the screen. You know just what that character looks like. You've got their posture down, know their facial expression and mannerisms. The scenery is described so perfectly you can practically smell the flowers and feel the cool winter wind sweeping across your face.

Good readers take time to make the words come alive on the page. They stop and notice and appreciate the language. Perhaps the descriptions will leap off the page and be powerful enough to be read aloud and shared, or be documented in a reading journal.

But unless we explicitly talk about the images we see as we are reading, they can be fleeting and dormant. Teachers need to lift up expressive text and talk about what they see in their heads when they read. A conversation may be started like this: "The author didn't say anything about a beard, but I see the preacher with one, what do you think? Is he the type of man who would have facial hair?"

It is just like when you've read a book and then go see the movie. Sometimes the director has cast the movie with our idea of the perfect characters! And we are *so* pleased! Other times, the plot is twisted a bit and it doesn't match what we thought as we were reading. Is it better to see the movie first, or read the book? I say read the book. Let your imagination have full reign and power. Savor the words. Movies often move too fast and lose the moments that were stretched beautifully by the author. Take time to talk about the pictures in your heads.

Listen to the Voice Inside Your Head

No, you are not schizophrenic! Inside *every* reader's head there is a little guy who is wide awake. He is alert and paying attention to every word your eyes read. He listens attentively piecing together the words and knocking on your brain whenever something strikes him. We rely on him to maximize our reading. This is his job! He might say,

"Hey, that didn't sound right, go back and reread that part!"

or

"Whoa, too many pronouns here, I've lost track of who *she* is! Go back a few paragraphs and reidentify the speaker."

or

"Time to get out a pencil to jot down the characters. I'm getting lost!"

or

"I have never seen or heard *that* word before—what could it mean?"

or

"Doesn't this remind me of something else I've read?"

or

"What beautiful writing this is. I can totally see this in my mind. Let's read it again."

or

"Something tells me the author just used foreshadowing. I'd better pay attention to that!"

or

"I think I've figured out what's going to happen. I need to talk to my friend who is also reading this book and share my thoughts!"

◎ *The list goes on and on. Good readers are constantly amplifying this voice in their heads. Good readers pay attention when that voice knocks. They* stop *their reading, pause and think. That is what reading is all about. Thinking. Reading is thinking. And our job is to teach our students and remind ourselves that it's not a race to see who finishes first. It's accessing that little voice, dialoguing with it and being a sharp, critical participant in the act of reading. And all along the way we need to be talking with other readers to deepen the process even further.*

Wake up that little voice in your head. He is your best friend in the reading process!

Author's Purpose

Author's purpose is *huge*. It's huge because not only do we need to get in an author's shoes and identify *why* the piece was written, but also when we ask kids to write, from the very beginning we want them to think like authors and establish *their* purpose!

One time I went to listen to a great speaker who began his talk by lifting up a stack of things he had read the day before. They included items such as a take out menu, a bus schedule, the comics, *Time* magazine, a cheesy novel, and the classified ads. Then he started his talk on author's purpose.

You get the idea. Below are three general categories of print. Authors write:

To Entertain	*To Inform*	*To Persuade*
comics	headline news	editorials
fantasy books	biographies	magazine ads
mysteries	bus schedules	campaign flier
poems	poems	poems

(Yes, poems, as well as many other genres like diaries can have multiple purposes.) Authors know *who* their audience is when they sit down and figure the angle they wish to take on their work. They know if they are trying to make the reader laugh, cry, sigh, consternate, or change their mind on a controversial topic. It's fun to always ask students, "Why do you think the author wrote this?" It will get them in the habit of thinking when reading, so when they sit down to write, they will ask the same about their own writing purpose!

Using a Bookmark

There are a plethora of uses for a bookmark. A bookmark is much more than a device to keep track of what page you're on. It's a handy tool for:

- keeping track of characters

- noting favorite words/phrases and the pages they're on

- marking similes/metaphors/alliteration/personification

- jotting down predictions

- highlighting confusing or new words

A Recipe Box of Books

Follow these steps to create a recipe box to keep track of the books you read.

1. Get a recipe box with dividers.

2. Label each divider with a different genre (e.g., historical fiction, mystery, science fiction, nonfiction, sports, fantasy, realistic fiction).

3. Use a 3-inch by 5-inch note card as a bookmark. When you finish the book, you can fill out the notecard and file it under the genre. (See Figure 7–2.)

All Mistakes Are *Not* Equal!

It is true. All readers make mistakes. Sometimes our brains are working ahead of our mouths and our minds. Sometimes we are thinking while

Figure 7–2

Note Card: Fiction and Nonfiction Format

Fiction Format

Title: _____

Author:_____

Characters:_____

Setting:_____

Problem: _____

Solution: _____

My reaction to the book: _____

_____

Nonfiction Format

Title:_____

Author:_____

Key Points:_____

_____

_____

_____

This makes me think about: _____

_____

we are reading and other times just *word calling* or saying the word without thinking if it makes sense. Consider the following sentence:

My mother wore perfume.

Here are two types of mistakes that could happen in a reader's mind with that sentence.

Mistake Type #1: The "Who Cares?" mistake.
My *mom* wore perfume.

The reader simply substituted a word that made sense. Error? Yes! But it didn't interfere with the meaning so it's a *good* mistake to make!

Mistake Type #2: The "It Matters!" mistake
My *monkey* wore perfume.

This reader substituted a word that made no sense. The story is not about a monkey! Most likely the reader saw the first two letters *m-o* and just substituted a word that looked the same. This is when we need to prompt and say, "Now, try that again!" or "Did that make sense?" A good reader will self-correct.

Remember, *comprehension* is the bottom line in reading!

Does It *Look* Right, *Sound* Right, and *Make Sense?*

Marie Clay from New Zealand is the founder of Reading Recovery, a very world renown intervention program for struggling readers. She coined the series of questions, "Does is *look* right, *sound* right, *make sense?*" These are *the* three questions we need to ask as readers wage their guess when they take a stab at an unknown word. Clay believes that if young readers internalize these three questions, then they will develop a self-extending system for solving unknown words.

As adults helping struggling readers, we need to resist the temptation to jump in and tell them the word with which they are struggling. Instead, we need to encourage them to think of *all* the tools they can use to solve for unknown words by themselves.

Try using these prompts:

"Do you know another word that *looks* like that?"

Knowing *look* will help access *shook*.

"Get your mouth ready. Say the first sound."

Sometimes it just takes the initial sound for the word to spill out.

"Look at the picture!"

In young readers' books, the illustration gives lots of clues to the meaning.

"Do you remember that word from another page?"

Flipping back and recognizing it from before will spark prior knowledge.

"Go the beginning of the sentence and try it again!"

Sometimes getting a jump-start is all it takes.

"Sound it out."

Although this doesn't work all the time (consider the words *have* and *gave*) sounding out words and taking them apart on the run can work many times.

"Is there a chunk you know?"

Knowing *-ing* can help solve the word *thing*.

"What would make sense?"

This is the *most important* question we want readers to ask! See the Tool Box below for guidelines.

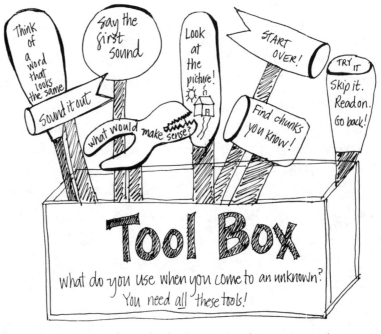

Figure 7–3

The H Brothers

The H Brothers!

Learning that two letters make just one sound is an eye-opening thing for young readers. If we treat the blends of *th, sh, ch,* and *wh* as brothers, students will remember their personalities and get excited whenever they encounter them in print.

TH

Th is the rude one. He is always sticking out his tongue. Try it! Say, *th*is, *th*at, *th*ose, *th*em, wi*th*, wea*th*er, toge*th*er, *th*oughtful, *Th*anksgiving. . . . Look in the mirror and exaggerate it; it's fun!

SH

Sh is well mannered. He is looking at *th* and telling him to "Sh . . . sh . . . sh!" Try these words! Say *sh*e, *sh*oe, *sh*ort, *sh*op, *sh*ip, *sh*ape, wi*sh*, ba*sh*ful.

CH

Ch is obsessed with trains. All day long he goes around the house saying "*Ch*oo! *Ch*oo! *Ch*ocolate *ch*ip cookies fuel his engine!"

WH

Wh is the clueless brother. He is always asking questions like "*wh*at?" "*wh*ere?" "*wh*en?" and "*wh*y?"

Good Readers Talk About What They Read

The most natural thing in the world is to share what we're reading with someone else. As good readers, we want and need to pass on our enthusiasm, our new learning, or our wonderings to someone else. There are so many ways to enjoy print together. Authors write their books with the intention that multitudes of people will read them and share thoughts. Here are some prompts to ignite conversation or correspondence.

- What was the funniest part?

- What was the scariest part?

- How did you like the ending?

- Did you predict what was going to happen?

- If you could turn this into a movie, who would you cast for each character?

- Who are you most like in this book?

- What surprised you the most?

- Did you ever get confused? Where?

- Find your favorite part and read it aloud!

- What does this make you think about?

You can think of more prompts. The idea is that reading is not meant to be a solitary activity. We ought to spend a few minutes savoring everything we read before moving on to our next text.

The Strainer in Your Brain

Books and articles can be so long! Reading can be such a tedious task if the reader pays equal attention to every detail.

Determining Importance in What We Read

It's a powerful visual image to think of our brain as a strainer. Your conversation may go something like this:

Tutor: *Picture this. You are cooking macaroni noodles on the stovetop in boiling water. The timer goes bing! So you carefully grab the hot pads, lift the heavy pot over to the sink and pour the scalding water into the _____. What do you call that thing? (Hopefully the student says strainer.)*

Tutor: *Yes! Describe it for me!*

Student: *Well it has holes in it so the water can go through and the noodles can stay inside.*

Tutor: *Perfect! You know, that's what good readers do too. Their brain acts like a strainer, draining off the minute details, or the water and saving the main ideas, the noodles. Let's try pulling out the noodles in what we read today!*

Coding the Text

This is a fabulous strategy to use to ensure engagement with print, particularly when reading informational text.

Students can either use the code that follows or they can make up their own original code, which gives them a special feeling of ownership.

! New information! Need to remember this!

? Huh? I don't get this!

☺ Cool! I already know this!

* This matters to me. Like a star in the sky, I want the message be lifted up!

If the text is a photocopy, then they can write right on the paper in the margins, highlighting or drawing arrows. If the text is not consumable, then sticky notes work equally well.

Scribing Your Voice

Remember that little guy who sits up in your brain and is talking to you as you read? Some people find it helpful to write down what that voice is saying as they are reading. Little sticky notes work perfectly for this. Students and tutors can work independently recording their voice-talk and then compare what their voices were saying at the end of the read.

The Y Chart

Clearly, the Y Chart is the most fabulous tool any reader can use on any content material from a picture book to any informational article to a chapter in a textbook or to *Gone with the Wind*! In order to really read proficiently, a good reader must do three things simultaneously:

1. Summarize

2. Make connections

3. Ask questions

This chart does it all on one page. It is recommended that you use a spiral notebook to keep the Y charts together. This is a wonderful way to track comprehension and access higher-thinking skills while engaging the reader. Though it slows the reading process down, it ensures connectivity with the text. It is best done during reading. Take the Y Chart back to a small group and presto, each member is ready to discuss!

Figure 7–4

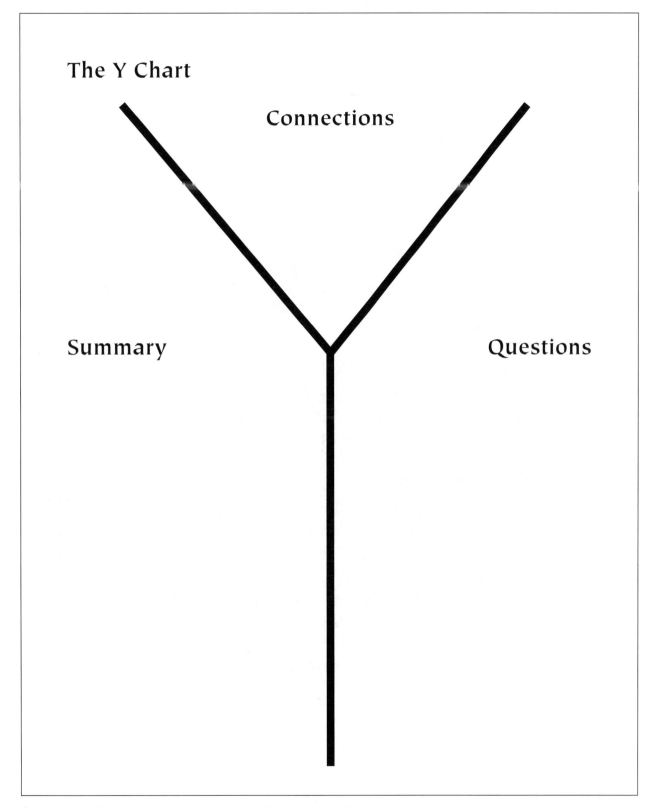

The Y Chart

Connections

Summary

Questions

CHAPTER 8

After Reading Activities

Reading and Writing Go Hand in Hand

Reading and writing are connected like an electrical circuit. The more we expose kids to all kinds of print, the more versatile, informed, and better readers they become. They absorb rich vocabulary, complex plot structures, nonfiction layout, and countless other things.

The energy from reading travels into their heart where they feel it. It goes into their stomach where they digest it. Instead of being passed through, however, it travels to their fingertips of their writing hand.

Place both hands on your head. In the left, hold a book—a book you love. In the right hand, hold a pencil or a computer keyboard. The weight of your hands rests on your brain where new original writing thoughts are ignited! The wealth of genres and writing styles have been stored up there in the brain and are ready to be tapped into as young writers emulate different writing styles.

Consider these truisms:

- "Better readers make better writers."

- "Writing floats on a sea of talk."

- "How do I know what I think until I see what I say?"

Sketch to Stretch

Use *sketch to stretch* as a different kind of approach to comprehension. This strategy helps students interpret texts to gain insights into the theme by shifting from reading to drawing. It is based on the premise that students will have additional insights when they change mediums (sketching instead of writing). The strategy has two parts:

1. Making a quick sketch following a short piece.

2. Sharing the sketch, discussing it.

Students read a text either silently or orally. Then they sketch what the piece meant to them *not* an illustration from the story. It is a quick sketch, not a piece of artwork. The tutor also sketches, keeping the drawings private.

When the quick sketches are complete, they are shared. The artist remains quiet while the other person interprets the meaning behind the sketch. A discussion ensues that takes the meaning to a higher level (hopefully!). *Note:* This is an *excellent* prewriting activity for a reflective follow-up.

The Summary Sentence

Being able to summarize a piece of text in one nitty-gritty sentence is critical. Too often we get bogged down in details. As a fun after-reading exercise, we can plug the most salient thoughts into the following formula to sift out the most important elements of a piece of text.

_____ wanted _____, but _____ so _____.

Here are two samples from familiar texts.

The Three Little Pigs

The wolf *wanted* to blow down the houses of the three little pigs, *but* they outsmarted him, *so* he ended up in a pot of boiling water!

Charlotte's Web

Charlotte *wanted* to save Wilbur's life, *but* Fern's father was serious about slaughtering him, *so* she spun mysterious words in her web to save his life.

For longer texts another model of the summary sentence is adding the word *then*.

There's a Boy in the Girl's Bathroom

Brad *wanted* stars next to his name on the chart in the classroom, *but* he was afraid his work wasn't good enough, *so* he didn't try. *Then* the school counselor changed his attitude.

T Chart

This is a fabulous tool for brainstorming, comparing, and weighing the sides of any issue. It can be used before reading, during reading, or after reading as a means to comprehend and connect with material. On one piece of paper the reader can synthesize information and document facts, thoughts, and beliefs. When kept in a spiral notebook for future reference, students have a powerful resource for persuasive writing pieces. If used often enough, it will become a natural tool for students to use when they encounter any genre or prompt. The T Chart (see Figure 8–1) trains the brain to look at things such as pros and cons, cause and effect, belief and proof. Its uses know no boundaries!

To expand the experience, add another column for a Triple T. This is an excellent graphic for interacting with factual texts.

Word Webs

Our language is so intricate! Words come from root words in exponential ways. Sometimes it's appropriate and fun to pick a little familiar word, put it in the middle of a page, and play with it to see all of the places it can take us. Prefixes and suffixes build amazing derivations. Follow the format shown in Figure 8–2 on a big piece of paper.

Figure 8–1

The T Chart and Triple T Chart

Solar Power

Advantages	Disadvantages

Fact	Question	Response

Figure 8–2

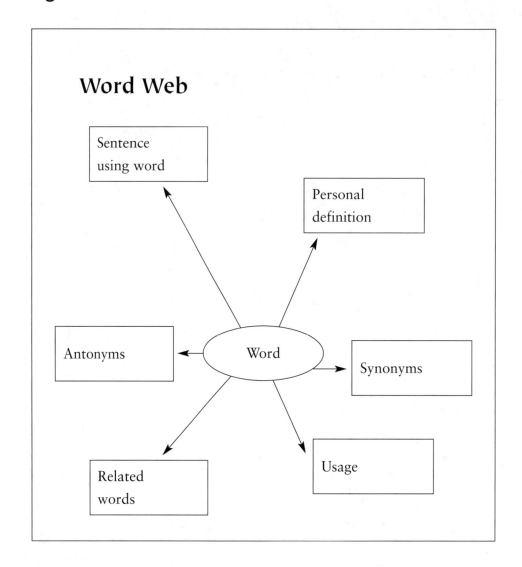

Words to Consider

happy: happiness, happier, unhappy, unhappiness, happiest

fat: fatter, fatty, fatten, fattening, unfattening, lowfat, fatso, fatted, fattest, nonfat, fats

agree: disagree, agreement, agreed, agreeing, agrees, disagreeing, disagreement, disagreeing

order: reorder, ordering, ordered, reordering, reorders, orders, disorder, disorderly

arrange: rearrange, arrangement, arranging, arranged, arranges, rearranging

art: artful, artsy, artist, artistically, artfully, artistic, artistry *place:* replace, placement, replacement, misplace, placing, placed, places, replaces, replacing

light: enlighten, enlightenment, lighting, lighter, lights, highlight, highlighted, highlighting, highlighter, lightening, lightly, lightest

love: unlovable, lovable, lover, lovely, unlovely, loving, loved, loves, beloved, unloving

I Am

This open-ended free verse can be used in so many ways. It invites insightful thinking. You can duplicate the form (see Figure 8–3) to use at the initial tutoring session to get know your student. You can also write one about yourself, as shown in Figure 8–4.

As you encounter different characters in fiction and nonfiction, it is fun to write in first person. These are quick writing opportunities that can be used to summarize characters and offer up varying viewpoints. It's a good, quick stretching exercise for the mind of the writer as well as the reader.

Syllable Soccer

A Vocabulary Reinforcement Game for Two

Purposes

- To reinforce segmenting words by chunks
- To familiarize common prefixes and suffixes
- To feel the word by clapping its syllables
- To use the word in context in a complete sentence
- To overcome fear of multisyllabic words
- To practice vocabulary words

Equipment

- game board (see Figure 8–5 on page 58)
- one game piece
- word cards (one word per card taken from student's reading or individual needs)

Figure 8–3

I Am

I am
I wonder
I hear
I see
I want
I am

I pretend
I feel
I touch
I worry
I cry
I am

I understand
I say
I dream
I try to
I hope
I am

Figure 8–4

I Am

I am really tired of cleaning.
I wonder if my mom knows how they are treating me.
I hear the mice squeaking.
I see them working like little seamstresses.
I want so badly to be normal.
I am not as ugly as I feel.

I pretend that nagging doesn't bother me.
I feel like this could be a miraculous evening.
I touch the pumpkin in disbelief.
I worry that I won't know when it's midnight.
I cry when I lose my shoe.
I am never going to be disheartened again.

I understand that everyone wants a handsome husband.
I say that miracles are possible.
I dream of dancing forever.
I try to keep smiling.
I hope he won't forget me.
I am Cinderella!

by Mary Wheeler

Figure 8–5 Syllable Soccer Game Board

SCORE! (upside down)

SYLLABLE ⚽ SOCCER

SCORE!

Rules

1. Put your game piece in the middle of the board.

2. Choose who goes first.

3. Player 1 draws a card, says and claps the word by syllables.

4. Player 1 says the word again and moves the game piece one space per syllable toward the opposing goal.

5. Player 1 then uses that word in a great sentence connecting with the plot of a book, a current event, or a connection to his/her life.

6. Player 2 then draws a card and repeats steps three through five moving his game piece toward the opposite goal.

7. A goal is scored when a player claps a word into the end zone.

   Game can be timed or end when someone scores.

The Power of Self-Reflection

You're deep into the plot and your stomach rumbles. *Ding!* The bell rings. You close the book. Hurry! On to lunch! Then math! No time to reflect!

But wait! This is important!

Have you stopped and thought about what you know that good readers do? Don't deprive yourself of this worthwhile discipline! Carve out some time to self-reflect. How are you doing? Are you:

Monitoring your comprehension?
Making predictions?
Making connections?
Making pictures in your head as you read?

Is your mind wandering while you read? Perhaps you need to be actively engaged with a highlighter in hand as in Figure 8–6. Maybe you should change your reading position, sit up straighter or get a brighter light. Another time of day may be better for your reading time. Would it help to have a bookmark to keep track of the characters? And don't forget the Y Chart! How is this text affecting you? What do you want to remember from it?

Figure 8–6

After Reading Report Card

Be Honest! Good readers are tuned into ALL of these things!

Did I ...	NOT VERY MUCH	A LITTLE BIT	MUCH OF THE TIM	ALL THE TIME
make predictions?				
create pictures in my head?				
make connections?				
stop and think if it got confusing?				
fix up my mistakes and understand it?				

Unless we stop to reflect, we will all be average readers. It is said that *great* is the enemy of *good*. Think about this as it refers to self-reflection. If we inflate our ability to read well, then we'll never grow as readers. Complacency makes us rot! Just like an untended garden, if we get sloppy with our reading habits, weeds will grow. We need to constantly assess ourselves and identify our reading tendencies. Let's stop skipping over words we don't know. Let's go back and reread the fuzzy parts, make notes in the margins, summarize as we go, and read the text with the same rigor in which it was written. Let's hold hands with the author. That's what good readers do.

Figure 8–7

Are You a Good Reader?

Read this passage quickly and see how you do!

The boys' arrows were nearly gone so they sat down on the grass and stopped hunting. Over at the edge of the wood they saw Henry making a bow to a small girl who was coming down the road. She had tears in her dress and tears in her eyes. She gave Henry a note which he brought over to the group of young hunters. Read to the boys it caused great excitement. After a minute, but rapid examination of their weapons, they ran down to the valley. Does were standing at the edge of the lake, making an excellent target.

What did you notice? What does this tell you about reading?

CHAPTER 9

Conclusion

You have said *yes!*

That little three-letter affirmative word holds more power and influence than you can even begin to imagine. You are soon to begin a volunteer effort that matters. You won't regret it. Somewhere out there in the world is a young person in need of an older person to help him along the way. You will be there in countless ways as you demystify the world of print.

Beginning each session with text from the outside world will set the tone for why we read. Your student will sit back as you share text from the real world of reading. Perhaps you will share a poem, or the front page of a newspaper, a take out menu, a picture book, or a passage out of the book you're reading. In any case, you will have time to discuss it, which is what real readers do in the real world. Then as you move into your student's text, he will show off by practicing familiar reading and thus increasing fluency. You will assist your student with new reading material, incorporate phonics, and move to a reading–writing connection. Through all of this, it is the bond between you that will strengthen. You will inevitably develop your own teaching style as time goes on. Don't be surprised if your tutoring time becomes one of your favorite times during the week. Because you are contributing in such a meaningful way, we hope that you spread the word to other friends and associates who are available and willing. Truly, no child should ever be left behind or fall through the cracks. Your efforts will be rewarded time and time again.

Hopefully you feel equipped to proceed with the heart of a motivated volunteer. May the words of poet Steven Layne (*Life's Literacy Lessons*) speak to you as you reach out in this venture.

Reading Orphans

Reading orphans,
We're out there you know.
Moved to many times, developmental delays,
Or maybe something just didn't click fast enough for the system.

It's amazing how we can be surrounded by other kids.
In a classroom year after year
And still feel alone, separate.

And the older we get, the greater the chasm.

We reading orphans look to you, our teachers,
Our one best hope for change.
You're frantic, frazzled, overworked, and underpaid.
We know.

But we look to you, still—

Using every attention seeking behavior we possess
We're sending you a coded message . . . .
Adopt us.

APPENDICES

Shape Your Thinking

DETERMINING IMPORTANCE

Three points I want to remember

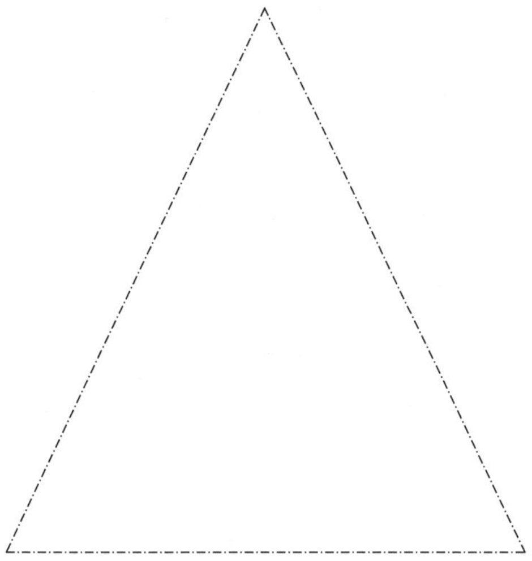

QUESTIONING

One issue that keeps circling around in my mind.

RELATING NEW TO KNOWN

Four ideas that "square" with my thinking.

A–1

Question Stem Cubes

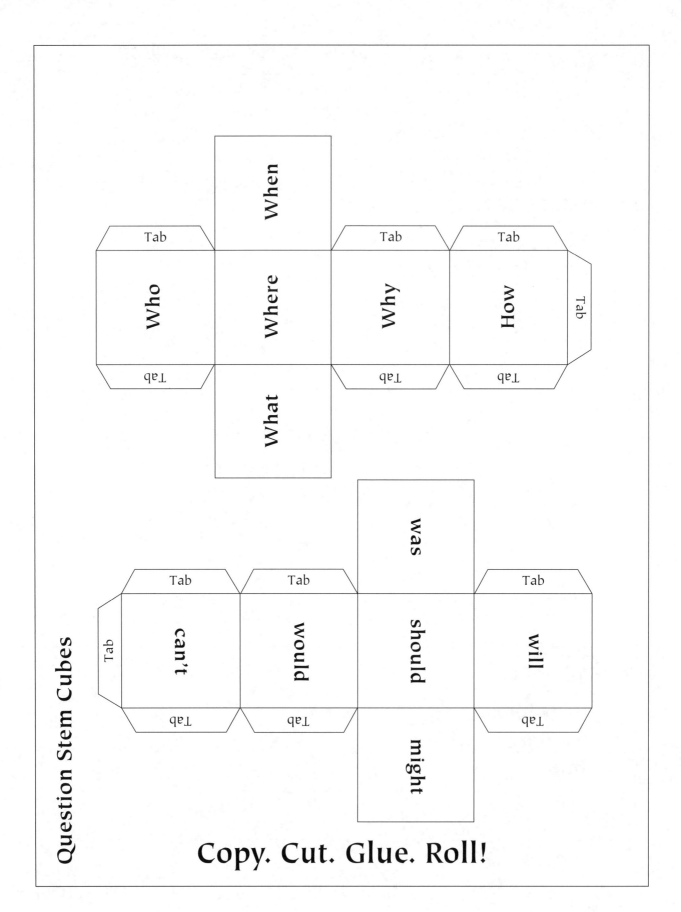

Copy. Cut. Glue. Roll!

When
Tab   Tab   Tab
Who   Where   Why   How   Tab
Tab   Tab   Tab
What

was
Tab   Tab   Tab
can't   would   should   will
Tab   Tab   Tab
might

Asking Questions

	Is	Did	Can	Would	Will	Might
Who?						
What?						
Where?						
Why?						
When?						
How?						

A–3

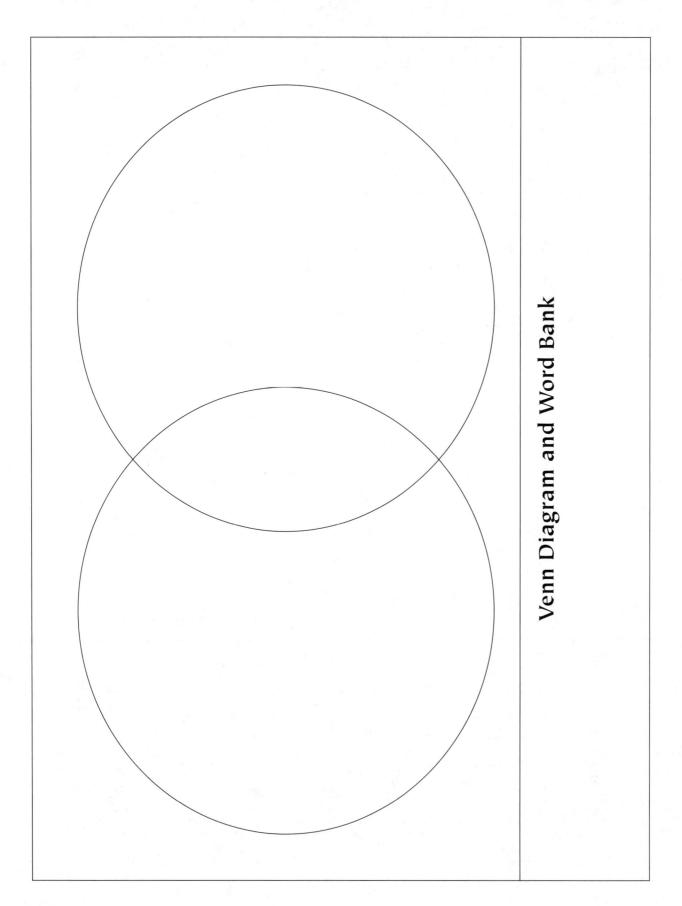

Venn Diagram and Word Bank

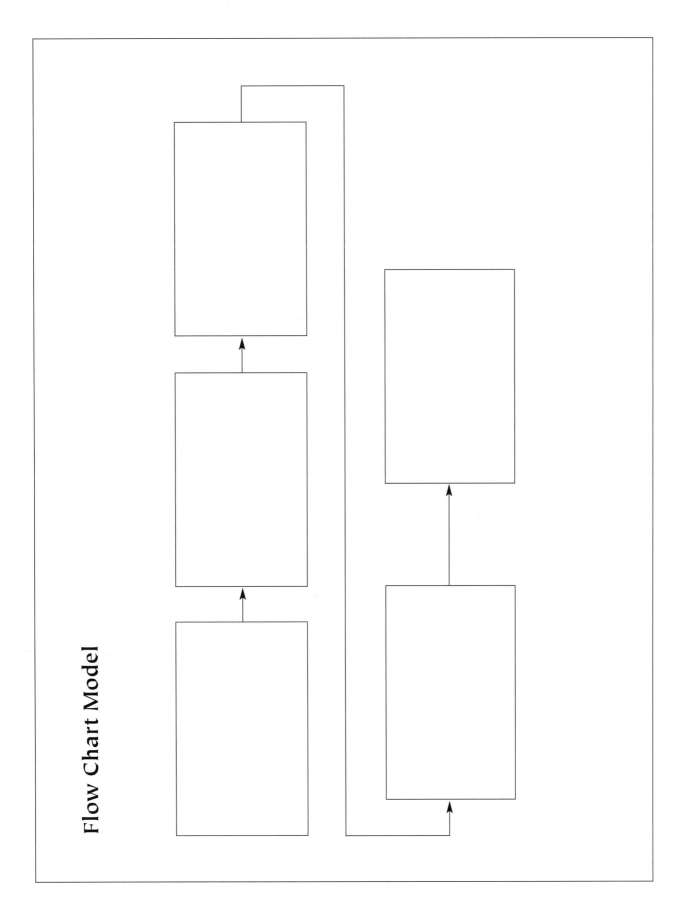

Flow Chart Model

Compare and Contrast

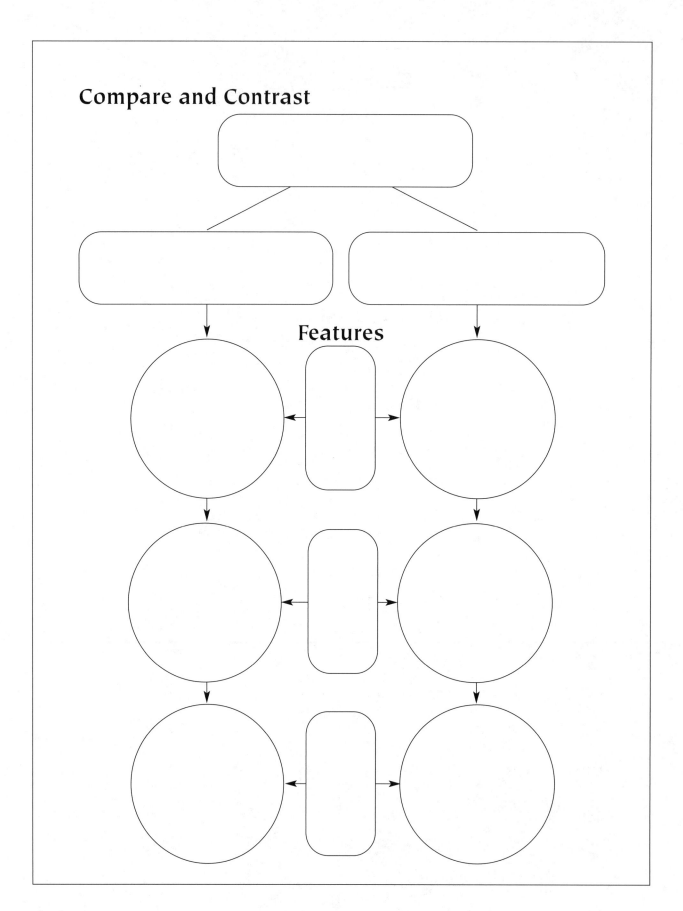

Features

Story Star

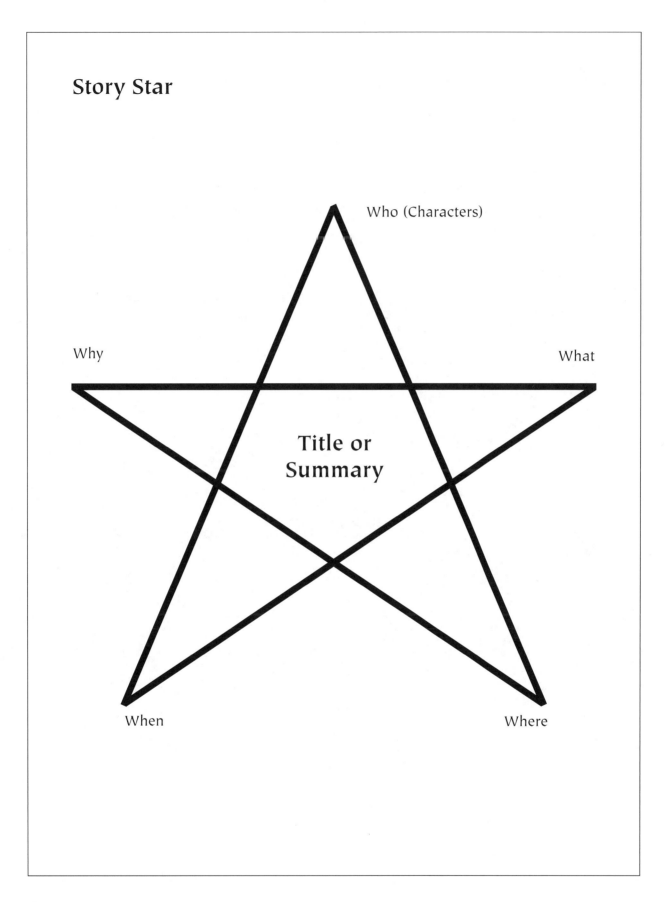

Herringbone Organizer

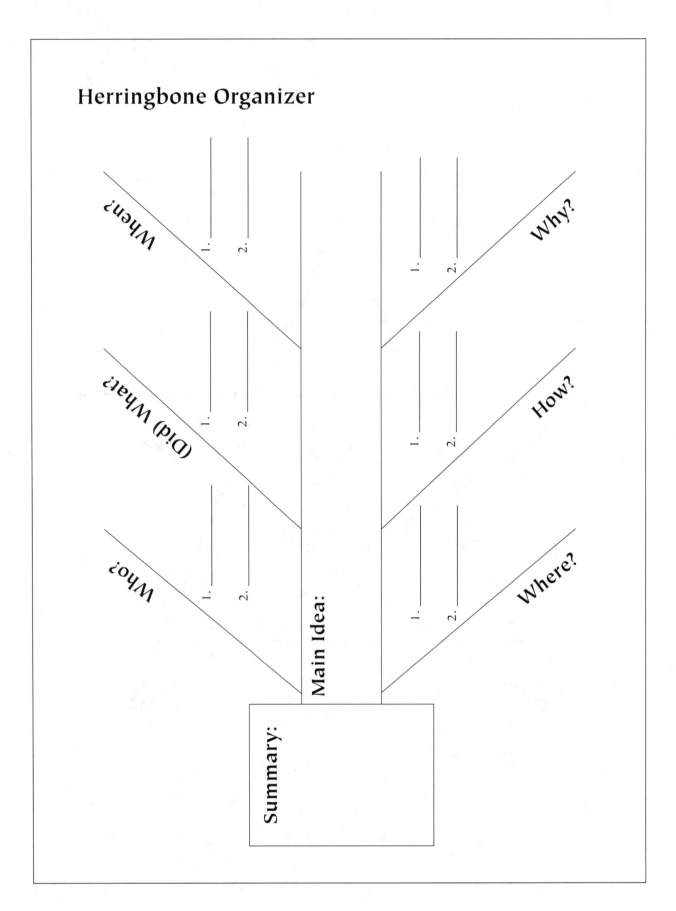

When?

(Did) What?

Who?

Why?

How?

Where?

1.
2.

1.
2.

1.
2.

1.
2.

1.
2.

1.
2.

Main Idea:

Summary:

Bubble Map

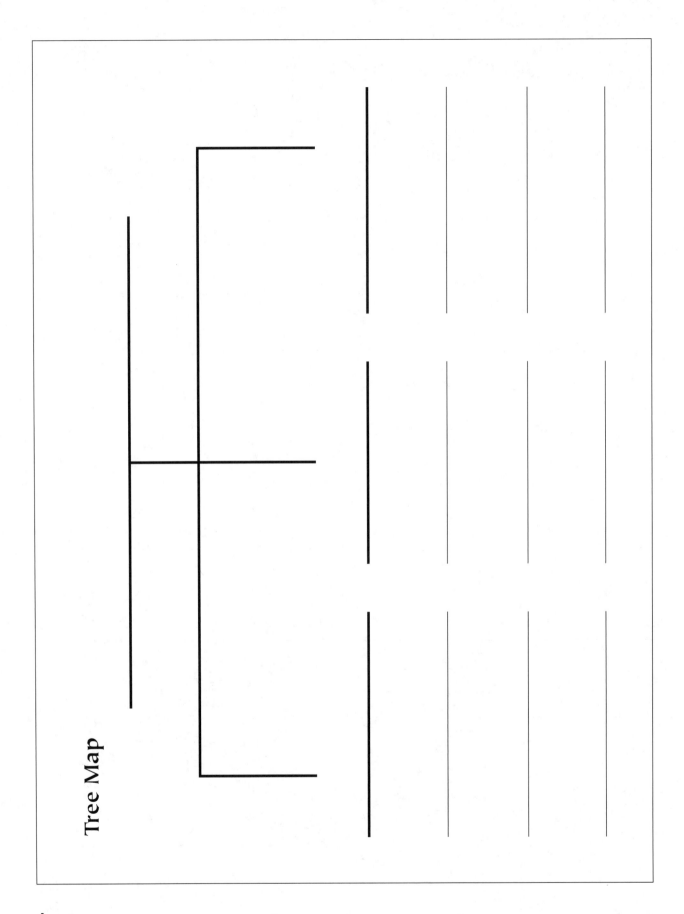

Tree Map

KWL Chart

What We Know	What We Want to Know	What We Learned

Viewpoints/Beliefs/Actions

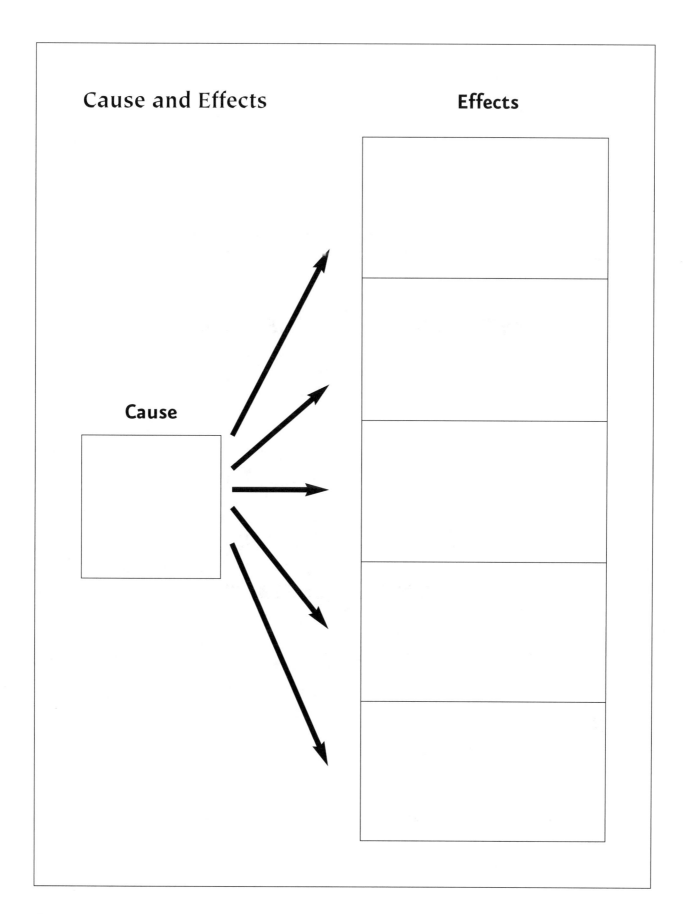

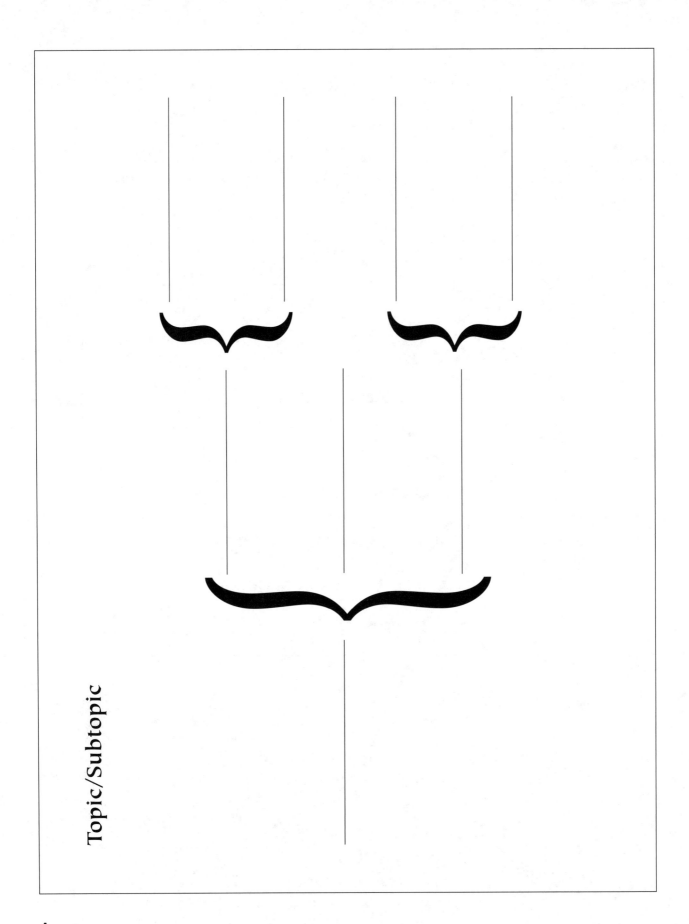

Topic/Subtopic

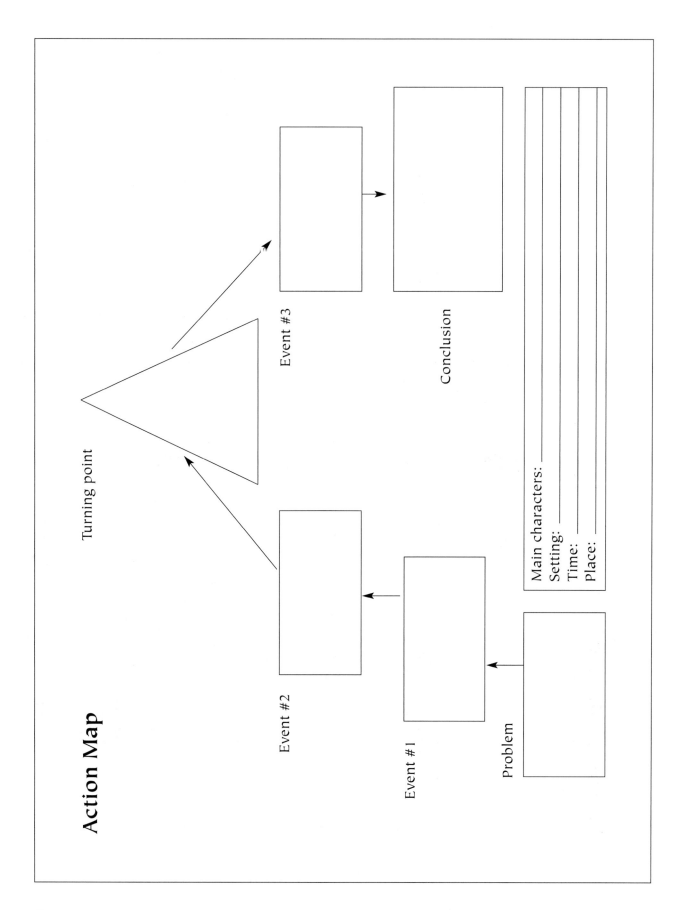

Action Map

Turning point

Event #3

Event #2

Conclusion

Event #1

Problem

Main characters: _____
Setting: _____
Time: _____
Place: _____

Problem/Solutions

The Problem:

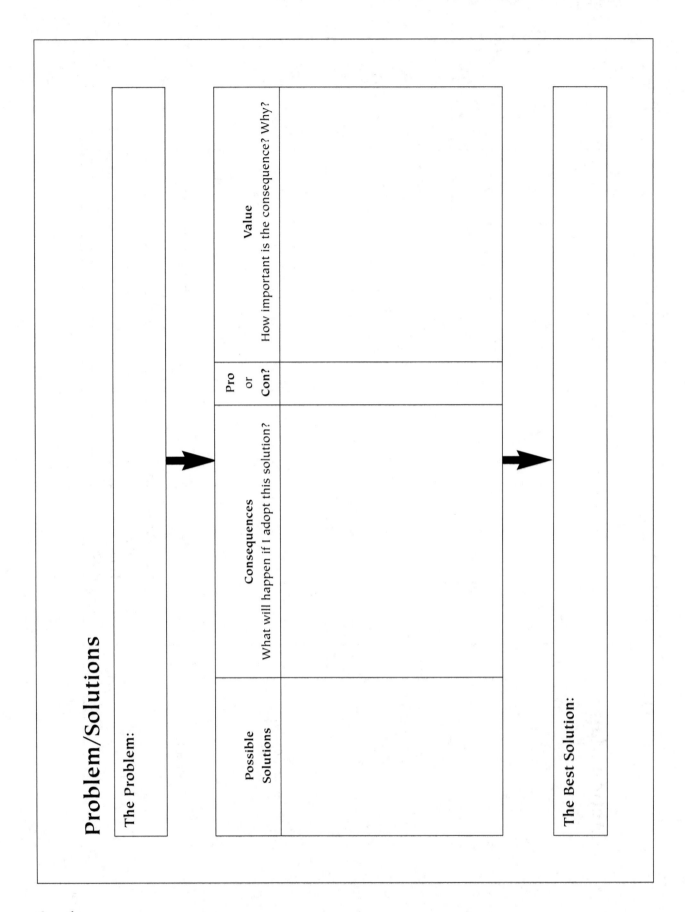

Possible Solutions	Consequences What will happen if I adopt this solution?	Pro or Con?	Value How important is the consequence? Why?

The Best Solution:

Storyboard

Goal: _____

_____

Include: Who, what, when, why, where, how

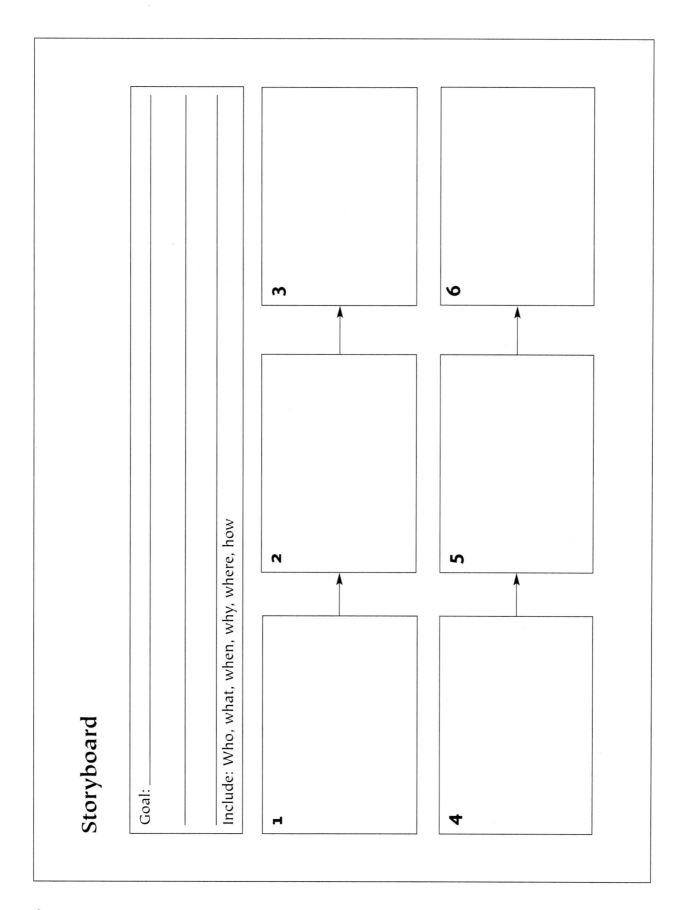

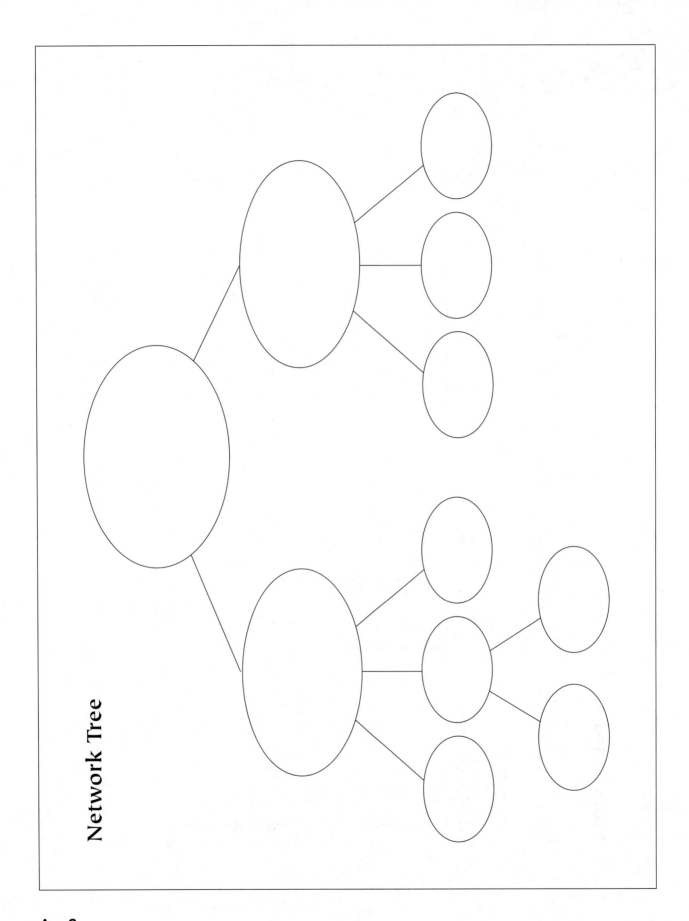

Network Tree

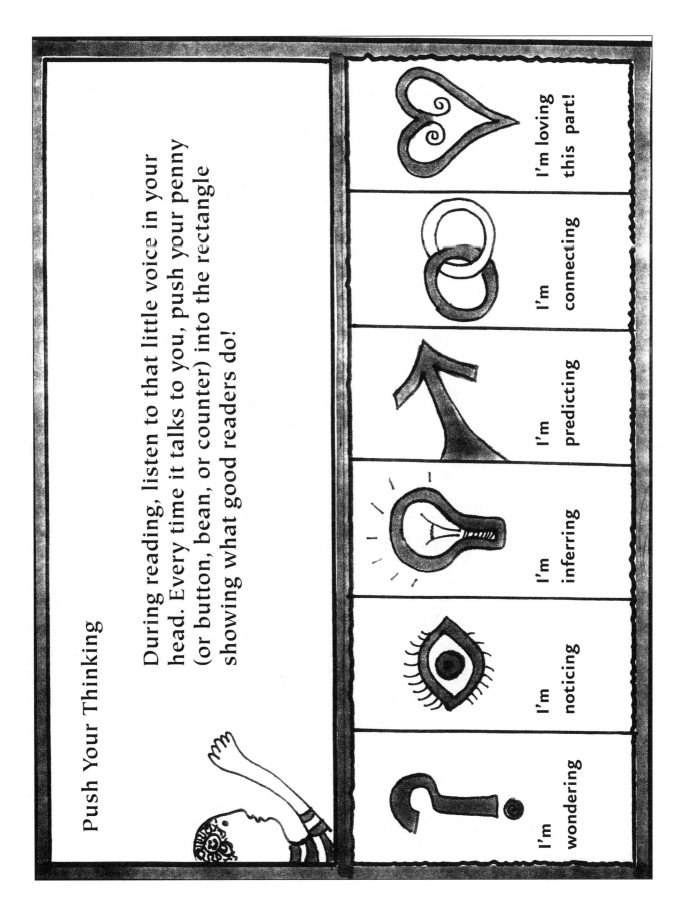

Push Your Thinking

During reading, listen to that little voice in your head. Every time it talks to you, push your penny (or button, bean, or counter) into the rectangle showing what good readers do!

I'm loving this part!

I'm connecting

I'm predicting

I'm inferring

I'm noticing

I'm wondering

A–19

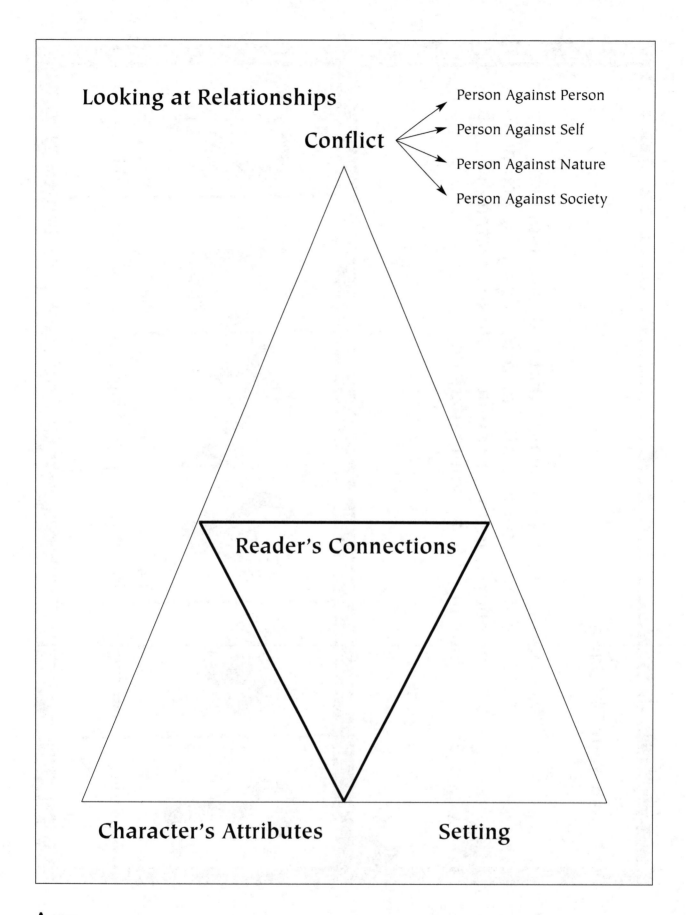

Looking at Relationships

Conflict
- Person Against Person
- Person Against Self
- Person Against Nature
- Person Against Society

Reader's Connections

Character's Attributes

Setting

A–20

Fact/Question/Response

Name _____

Text _____

FACT	QUESTION	RESPONSE

Get to Know You Inventory

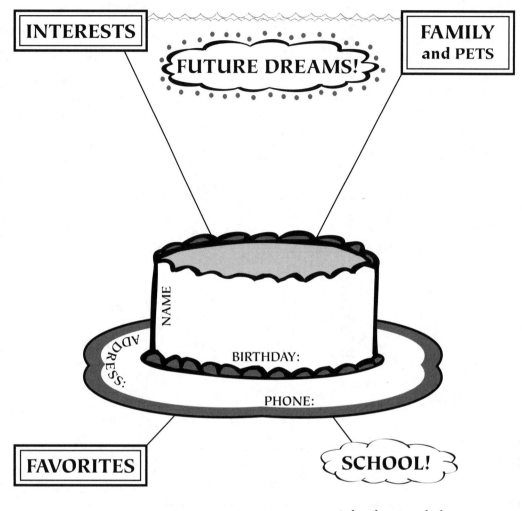

INTERESTS

FUTURE DREAMS!

FAMILY and **PETS**

NAME

ADDRESS:

BIRTHDAY:

PHONE:

FAVORITES

SCHOOL!

song:
book:
restaurant:
things to do alone:
room in the house:
heroes:
subject:
places:

Schools attended:

Memorable teachers:

Memorable times:

Memorable friends:

Individual Word Wall

Aa	Bb	Cc	Dd
Ee	Ff	Gg	Hh
Ii	Jj	Kk	Ll
Mm	Nn	Oo	Pp

Qq	Rr	Ss	Tt
Uu	Vv	Ww	Xx
Yy	Zz	Spelling Patterns	Spelling Patterns
Spelling Patterns	Spelling Patterns	Spelling Patterns	Spelling Patterns

A–23 *Continued*

Common Sight Words

the	day	were	take	found	sat
and	at	ask	eat	lady	stay
a	have	back	body	soon	each
I	your	now	school	ran	ever
to	mother	friend	house	dear	until
said	come	cry	morning	man	shout
you	not	oh	yes	better	mama
he	like	Mr.	after	through	use
it	then	bed	never	stop	turn
in	get	an	or	still	thought
was	when	very	self	fast	papa
she	thing	where	try	next	lot
for	do	play	has	only	blue
that	to	let	always	am	bath
is	want	long	over	began	mean
his	did	here	again	head	sit
but	could	how	side	keep	together
they	good	make	thank	teacher	best
my	this	big	why	sure	brother
of	don't	from	who	says	feel
on	little	put	saw	ride	floor
me	if	read	mom	pet	wait
all	just	them	kid	hurry	tomorrow
be	baby	as	give	hand	surprise
go	way	Miss	around	hard	shop
can	there	any	by	push	run
with	every	right	Mrs.	our	own
one	went	nice	off	their	
her	father	other	sister	watch	
what	had	well	find	because	
we	see	old	fun	door	
him	dog	night	more	us	
no	home	may	while	should	
so	down	about	tell	room	
out	got	think	sleep	pull	
up	would	new	made	great	
are	time	know	first	gave	
will	love	help	say	does	
look	walk	grand	took	car	
some	came	boy	dad	ball	

Adapted from M. Eeds. 1985. "Bookwords: Using a Beginning Word List of High Frequency Words from Children's Literature K–3." *The Reading Teacher* 38: 420.

A–24

Prefixes/Meanings/Examples

Prefix	Meaning	Examples
a-, an-	not or without	anonymous
ab-	away from, off	absent, abandon
ad-	to	admit
amphi-	both, around	amphibious, amphitheater
bene-	well, good	benefit, benefactor
co-	together	coordinate, cooperate
dis-	opposite	dishonest, disagree
ex-	out	exit, extinguish
im-	not	impossible
mis-	wrongly, bad	mistake, misconception
pre-	before	preview, prefix
re-	back, again	revoke, review
sub-	under	submarine, submerge
super-	above, beyond	superficial, superintendent
trans-	across	transcend, transport
un-	not	unreal, unable, unfounded

Suffix	Meaning	Examples
-able	able to	portable, curable, believable
-crat	to rule	democrat, aristocrat
-ee, -eer	one who	employee, volunteer
-er	more	wiser, harder, stronger
-est	most	wisest, hardest, strongest
-less	without	fearless, careless, hopeless
-logy, -ology	study of	biology, psychology
-ly	having the quality of	manly, motherly, miserly
-ness	state, quality	happiness

Adapted from Janet Allen (1999). *Words, Words, Words*. Reprinted with permission.

A–25

Book Title	Author
Making Connections (grades K–2)	
Arthur's New Puppy	Marc Brown
A Color of His Own	Leo Lionni
Ira Sleeps Over	Bernard Waber
Koala Lou	Mem Fox
My Friend Rabbit	Eric Rohmann
Nana Upstairs, Nana Downstairs	Tomie de Paola
The Snowy Day	Ezra Jack Keats
William's Doll	Charlotte Zolotow
Making Connections (grades 3–5)	
Amazing Grace	Mary Hoffman
Brave Irene	William Steig
The Chalk Box Kid	Clyde Robert Bull
Dinner at Aunt Connie's House	Faith Ringgold
Going Home	Eve Bunting
The Relatives Came	Cynthia Rylant
Drawing Inferences (grades K–2)	
Alexander Who Used to Be Rich Last Sunday	Judith Viorst
Anna Banana and Me	Erik Lenore Blegvad
Corduroy	Don Freeman
In a Small, Small Pond	Pamela Allen
Noisy Nora	Rosemary Wells
Owen	Kevin Henkes
Rainbow Fish	Marcus Pfister
Swimmy	Leo Lionni
Drawing Inferences (grades 3–5)	
Charlie Anderson	Barbara Abercrombie
Once Upon MacDonald's Farm	Stephen Gammell
See the Ocean	Estelle Condra
The Stranger	Chris Van Allsburg
Teammates	Peter Golenback
The Wall	Eve Bunting

B–1

Book Title	Author
Visualizing (appropriate for all grade levels)	
Barn Dance	Bill Martin
Little Mouse's Painting	Diane Wolkstein
Night in the Country	Cynthia Rylant
Owl Moon	Jane Yolan
The Seasons of Arnold's Apple Tree	Gail Gibbons
Seven Blind Mice	Ed Young
The Trip	Ezra Jack Keats
Predictable Books (grades K–2)	
Are You My Mother?	P.D. Eastman
Brown Bear, Brown Bear	Bill Martin
The Gingerbread Boy	Paul Galdone
I Went Walking	Sue Williams
If You Give a Mouse a Cookie	Laura Numeroff
The Important Book	Margaret Wise Brown
Mrs. Wishy-Washy	Joy Cowley
The Napping House	Audrey Wood
The Very Hungry Caterpillar	Eric Carle
More Great Picture Books	
Alexander and the Terrible, Horrible, No Good, Very Bad Day	Judith Viorst
Arthur's Chicken Pox (or any Arthur books by Marc Brown)	Marc Brown
A Chair for My Mother	Vera Williams
A Day's Work	Eve Bunting
Frederick	Leo Lionni
Frog and Toad Are Friends	Arnold Lobel
Ira Sleeps Over	Bernard Weber
Lily's Purple Plastic Purse	Kevin Henkes
The Memory String	Eve Bunting
Miss Nelson Is Missing	Harry Allard
Pink and Say	Patricia Polacco
The Other Side	Jaqueline Woodson

B–1 *Continued*